Another Animal: Poems

A Cage of Spines

To Mix With Time: New & Selected Poems

Poems to Solve

Half Sun Half Sleep

Iconographs

More Poems to Solve

Windows & Stones:
Selected Poems of Tomas Tranströmer
(translated from the Swedish)

The Guess & Spell Coloring Book

New & Selected Things Taking Place

IN OTHER WORDS

In Other Words

MAY SWENSON

NEW POEMS

1 9  8 7

ALFRED A. KNOPF   NEW YORK

Copyright © 1979, 1980, 1981, 1982, 1983, 1984, 1986, 1987 by
May Swenson

All rights reserved under International and Pan-American Copyright
Conventions. Published in the United States by Alfred A. Knopf, Inc.,
New York, and simultaneously in Canada by Random House of Canada
Limited, Toronto. Distributed by Random House, Inc., New York.

Some poems in this work were originally published in the following
publications: *The Atlantic Monthly, Beyond Baroque Magazine, The
Buffalo News, Harvard Magazine, A Just God, The Nation, The New
Yorker, The Paris Review, Parnassus,* and *Portfolio One.*

The poem "Under the Baby Blanket" was originally published in
Antaeus.

The poems "Blood Test," "Dummy, 51, to Go to Museum," "A Day
Like Rousseau's *Dream,*" and "Saguaros Above Tucson" were originally published in *Poetry.*

Grateful acknowledgment is made to the following for permission to
reprint previously published material: *Birkhauser Boston Inc.:* "The
Cross Spider" by May Swenson from the anthology *Science '85 Songs
from Unsung Worlds.* Reprinted by permission of Birkhauser Boston
Inc. and the American Association for the Advancement of Science.
Bits Press, Case Western Reserve University: "Innards" by May Swen-
son from the anthology *Light Year '86.* Copyright © 1985 by May
Swenson. "A Nosty Fright" by May Swenson from the anthology
Light Year '84. Copyright © 1983, 1985 by May Swenson.

Library of Congress Cataloging-in-Publication Data

Swenson, May.
In other words.

I. Title.
PS3537.W478615   1987   811'.54   87-45118
ISBN 0-394-56175-9

Manufactured in the United States of America
FIRST EDITION

TO ROZANNE KNUDSON

CONTENTS

ONE

TWO

ONE

IN FLORIDA

Certain nasturtiums of that color, the gecko's neck
of urgent orange, a bubble he inflates until transparent,
then flattens, lets collapse. His intermittent goiter
swells, withdraws, pulls tight, and orange pimples
prick along his length. He's humping up and down,
announcing for a mate. She's not in sight.
Somnolent, gray as a dead twig he's been until today, stuck
on a plank of the porch. Or pale, hanging from splayed
toes on the hot stucco wall. Startling, his fat cravat
that bloats and shrinks, his belly of suede sheen, apricot.

Florida screams with colors, soft blooms, sharp juices, fruits.
Day-Glo insects jitter across the eye. A zebra butterfly
in strong sun trails an aura silver and black, like migraine.
Orchid, called Bull Hoof, flares by the fence, and Divi-Divi's
curled pods, feathery foliage effervesces out of a hollow.
Ylang-Ylang, the perfume tree, spreads cadmium-scented plumes.
Hydrangea, Mimosa, Guava, Loquat, Spanish Lime, Poinciana
to follow. Extravagant blushes of bushes, blossom-dressed
trees are a crowd in the yard. Slim palm trunks arch up and
curve like tall sway-necked flamingos.

Fruit of the Queen Palm peeled to the pit discloses miniature
monkey faces. Graceful, straight, the smooth pole of the Date
nests its fruit in clusters of ten thousand flowerets. This
the palm of which Mohammed said to the Arabs, "Honor her,
for she is your Mother." And Pawpaw and Possumwood grow
near Mango's cerise hairy flowers formed at each branch tip.
Giant leaves of the leaning Plantain, whose slatted canopies

make shade for the stiff bunched fruit called "fingers,"
each bunch finally to expand to a whole plump hand.

Two nights ago, under the porch that pokes a little way into
this tame jungle, six kittens slid out of the white cat, Polar.
Scarcely larger than mice, they're fixed to her teats,
where she lies spread for them like an odalisque. Five are
white as she, except for variant sooty noses, ears or tails.
The sixth, runt of the litter, the only male and pitch black,
has been nudged aside. He sucks on a sibling's ear mistaken
for a spigot. To behold the tableau, get on your knees,
put an eye to the widest crack between boards, where Polar
in the half-dark with her brood patiently endures.

A moment more, and she shakes herself loose from her blind
wriggling kits, crawls out from under to stand and stretch,
gardenia-white in dawn light on the porch, expecting
breakfast. Not far from a kitten herself, with her asking
purr, pink nose and slit green eyes, she crouches, laps her
milk, tugged teats hanging, heavy berries, in her belly's fur.

WATERBIRD

Part otter, part snake, part bird the bird Anhinga,
jalousie wings, draped open, dry. When slack-
hinged, the wind flips them shut. Her cry,
a slatted clatter, inflates her chin-
pouch; it's like a fish's swim-
bladder. Anhinga's body, otter-
furry, floats, under water-
mosses, neck a snake with white-
rimmed blue round roving eyes. Those long feet stilt-
paddle the only bird of the marsh that flies
submerged. Otter-
quick over bream that hover in water-
shade, she feeds, finds fillets among the water-
weeds. Her beak, ferrule of a folded black
umbrella, with neat thrust impales her prey.
She flaps up to dry on the crooked, look-
dead-limb of the Gumbo Limbo, her tan-
tipped wing fans spread, tail a shut fan dangled.

THREE WHITE VASES

A Sunday in June.
The water's clear
cornflower blue,
the sky its mirror.

Distinctly clear
the opposite coast,
its chalky sands
and miniature pavilions.

A flock of yachts,
midwater, distant,
spins. Near shore,
under my eye,

the waves are dark
blue, mussel-dyed,
where kids on a raft
teeter, splash, and

dive. Slippery bodies
climb up into sun
on the hot white planks.
Agile little hips

all wear different-
colored stripes.
As do the dinky
Sunfish setting out

tippily until,
taken in charge
by tiller and rein,
the spunky scraps

of sails snap tight
and slant on the wind.
A speedboat scampers
arcs of white spray,

a white pontoon plane
putt-putts, puts down
into choppy furrows
of the bay.

Uniquely bright,
the light today
reveals the scene
as through a pane

that's squeegee-clean.
White as the white
catamarans bobbing,
gulls on black-tipped

wings skid over.
My eye follows
to where they land.
On a lonely, reedy patch

of sand I see three
white vases stand,
each differently shaped:
one upright neck,

one hunched, the third
with neck downcurved.
Each fixed eye, intent,
watches what flinches

just under waveskin:
big school of tiny
glinting baitfish
spread on the bay.

The parents, that pair
of snowies, had a nest
in the eelgrass
all spring. The third

bird, the whitest,
is their child,
looks like a bud vase,
that long neck.

I see him
unhinge his slim
bill, wilt his neck.
I see the white

snaky throat
of the young egret
capably squirm
a blade-thin fish down.

STRAWBERRYING

My hands are murder-red. Many a plump head
drops on the heap in the basket. Or, ripe
to bursting, they might be hearts, matching
the blackbird's wing-fleck. Gripped to a reed
he shrieks his ko-ka-ree in the next field.
He's left his peck in some juicy cheeks, when
at first blush and mostly white, they showed
streaks of sweetness to the marauder.

We're picking near the shore, the morning
sunny, a slight wind moving rough-veined leaves
our hands rumple among. Fingers find by feel
the ready fruit in clusters. Here and there,
their squishy wounds. . . . Flesh was perfect
yesterday. . . . June was for gorging. . . .
sweet hearts young and firm before decay.

"Take only the biggest, and not too ripe,"
a mother calls to her girl and boy, barefoot
in the furrows. "Don't step on any. Don't
change rows. Don't eat too many." Mesmerized
by the largesse, the children squat and pull
and pick handfuls of rich scarlets, half
for the baskets, half for avid mouths.
Soon, whole faces are stained.

A crop this thick begs for plunder. Ripeness
wants to be ravished, as udders of cows when hard,
the blue-veined bags distended, ache to be stripped.
Hunkered in mud between the rows, sun burning

the backs of our necks, we grope for, and rip loose
soft nippled heads. If they bleed—too soft—
let them stay. Let them rot in the heat.

When, hidden away in a damp hollow under moldy
leaves, I come upon a clump of heart-shapes
once red, now spiderspit-gray, intact but empty,
still attached to their dead stems—
families smothered as at Pompeii— I rise
and stretch. I eat one more big ripe lopped
head. Red-handed, I leave the field.

BLOOD TEST

Alien, the male, and black. Big like a bear.
Wearing whitest clothes, of ironed cotton scalded clean.

I sat in a chair. He placed my arm on a narrow
tray-table bound in towel. As if to gut a fish.

"Mine the tiniest veins in the world," I warned.
He didn't care. "Let's see what we have," he said.

Tourniquet tied, he tapped his finger-ends inside
my elbow, smartly slapped until the thready vein fattened.

Didn't hurt. He was expert. Black chamois wrist and hand,
short square-cut nails, their halfmoons dusky onyx.

I made a fist. He slid the needle, eye-end in, first try,
then jumped the royal color into the tube.

Silence. We heard each other breathe. Big paw
took a tuft of cotton, pressed where the needle withdrew.

"That's it!" Broad teeth flashed. Eyes under bushy
mansard hair admired, I thought, that I hadn't flinched.

I got up. Done so quick, and with one wounding. I'd as soon
have stayed. To be a baby, a bearcub maybe, in his arms.

BIRTHDAY BUSH

Our bush bloomed, soon dropped
its fuchsia chalices. Rags
on the ground that were luscious
cups and trumpets, promises and brags.

A sprinkle of dark dots showed entry
into each silk cone. Down among
crisp pistils thirsty bumblebees
probed. Buds flared in a bunch

from tender stems. Sudden
vivid big bouquets
appeared just before our birthdays!
A galaxy our burning bush,

blissful explosion. Brief
effusion. Brief as these
words. I sweep away a trash
of crimson petals.

UNDER THE BABY BLANKET

Under the baby blanket 47 years old you are
asleep on the worn too-short Leatherette sofa.

Along with a watermelon and some peaches from
the beach cottage, you brought home this gift

from your Mom. "Just throw it in the van," you
said you said, "I haven't time to talk about it."

She had wanted to tell how she handstitched and
appliquéd the panels—a dozen of them—waiting

for you to be born: 12 identical sunbonneted
little girls, one in each square, in different

colors of dresses doing six different things.
And every tiny stitch put in with needle and

thimble. "It had to take months, looks like,"
I said. "Well, Mom's Relief Society ladies

must have helped," you said. One little girl
is sweeping, one raking, another watering a plant

in a pot, one dangling a doll dressed exactly
like herself. One is opening a blue umbrella.

At center is a little girl holding a book, with
your initial on the cover! I was astonished:

"A Matriarchal Blessing, predicting your future!"
(But, wait a minute, I thought. How did she know

you wouldn't be a boy? Was she also sewing
another blanket, with little boys in its squares:

holding hammer, riding tricycle, playing with
dog, batting ball, sailing boat, and so on?)

I asked for the baby blanket—which *is* a work
of art—to be hung on the wall above the sofa

where I could study it. You refused. You
lay down under it, bare legs drawn up, a smudge

of creosote on one knee. Almost covered with
little girls 47 years old you've gone to sleep.

DOUBLE EXPOSURE

Taking a photo of you taking a photo of me, I see
the black snout of the camera framed by hair, where

your face should be. I see your arms and one hand
on the shutter button, the hedge behind you and

beyond, below, overexposed water and sky wiped white.
Some flecks out of focus are supposed to be boats.

Your back toward what light is left, you're not
recognizable except by those cutoff jeans that I

gave you by shooting from above, forgetting your
legs. So, if I didn't know, I wouldn't know who

you are, you know. I *do* know who, but you, you know,
could be anybody. My mistake. It was because I

wanted to trip the shutter at the exact moment you
did. I did when you did, and you did when I did.

I can't wait to see yours of me. It's got to be
even more awful. A face, facing the light, pulled up

into a squint behind the lens, which must reflect
the muggy setting sun. Some sort of fright mask

or Mardi Gras monster, a big glass Cyclopean eye
superimposed on a flattened nose, that print,

the one you took of me as I took one of you. Who,
or what, will it be—will *I* be, I wonder? Can't wait.

DUMMY, 51, TO GO TO MUSEUM
VENTRILOQUIST DEAD AT 75

Charlie didn't want to be pushed down
that last time into his plush-lined
case, top hat and monocle removed,
head unscrewed, clever hinge of wooden
jaw detached, the lid snapped shut
and locked, for transmigration to the
Smithsonian. That night, in Bergen's
bedroom, Charlie, in his box, got
himself together by himself and squawked:
"Edgar! You can't make me leave you.
You can't live without me. I'm your
larynx and your tongue. You'd be dumb
without your dummy, Dummy!" Bergen,
stung by that urbane, impudent, bossy,
caustic and beloved voice, silently
swallowed a pearl shirtstud of Charlie's,
spiked with strychnine. Obediently,
Edgar died in his sleep. In the dark
of dislocation, Charlie, glass-eyed, tried
all by himself to weep. A tear of wood
formed and stood in the inner corner
of his left eye, but could not fall.

A THANK-YOU LETTER

Dear Clifford: It took me half an hour
to undo the cradle of string in which
your package from Denmark came.

The several knots tied under, over and
athwart each other—tightly tied and looped
and tied again—proved so perplexing. When,

finally, the last knot loosened, letting
the string—really a soft cord—fall free,
the sense of triumph was delicious.

I now have this wonderful cord 174″ long
although your package is only 13 x 10 x 2.
Of course I could have cut through

each juncture of the cat's cradle you
trussed the package into, and freed it
instantly. But, no! Cord like this,

strong, flexible, just tough enough, smooth
and blond, of twisted strands of rag or hemp,
is very rare here. In fact I haven't seen

the sort since childhood. Instead, we get
slick, scratchy, recalcitrant nylon, or
whatever, that's heavy or else thread-thin

and cuts your hands. It doesn't hold—
doesn't hold a knot, not one!
Right now, Boa, our cat, has harnessed

herself and is rolling over with several
wraparounds of your string. She's getting up
to gallop, ensnarling herself worse. She's

having a wonderful puzzle-playtime. Cat's
in her cradle, on her back, trying to bite
string off her claws. And I haven't yet

taken the sturdy paper off your package.
I hardly feel I want to. The gift has been
given! For which, thank you ever so much.

TEDDY'S BEARS

Skins on the floors, skins flung on the chairs,
and stretched on the walls of nearly every room.
Along with trophy-heads of buffalo, moose and deer,
tusks and toothy snarls of lioness and tiger.
But, most of all, bears.
Great and small furs, belly down, flat on the floor,
teeth and claws real, fully dimensional, as if clicking.
By the bed, this head: a lump with leather nose,
garnet eyes, jaws open, saber canines exposed.
And the rug in the gunroom on the third floor
is the biggest bear you've ever seen. Hod-sized head
with the round ears nearly worn away, wide goldbrown
body. Down the hall, across the railing of a doorway
where the plaque says PLAYROOM, are three Teddy Bears,
small, medium and large, at tea around a table
with an elaborately gowned cloth Lady Doll and her
china baby. A fourth plump Teddy forks a rockinghorse
in the corner.
Descending the stairs, you can't help but pause and fix
on the large portrait, life-sized, that's hung in the
stairwell: Poised rampant, the tanned Rough Rider,
wide-cuffed gloved hands pressed on the hilt of his sword,
squared head on short neck, chin raised, eyes piercing
rimless spectacles, lips under shaggy mustache in a stern
but amiable smile—the actual Teddy Himself.

ALTERNATE SIDE SUSPENDED

On wall-to-wall rugging the cars slouch by,
with headlights groping, windows blind,
the drivers invisible in the blizzard.

By morning, stalled at curbside, rounded high
as marriage beds, or frosty coffins, the piled
tops show carved hew-marks made by wind.

"Alternate side suspended," the city is numb.
Slabs on windowsills, like rocksalt, stay
unmelted three days, before beginning to gray

and shrink under sun. By now, the street's
soft corridor, gritty and scuffed, is dirtied
by dogs and the snowball wars of boys.

So begins the digging out. Windshields scraped,
engines strain, exhausts from tailpipes soil
a once spotless rug. Old asphalt potholes

show through. Eight o'clock walkers-to-work
pick paths past plastic hills of frozen
garbage, cheerfully splatter through slush, glad

for the noise and cram of harsh-colored cars,
horns hooting, drivers swearing, the street
steaming as usual under a urine-yellow sun.

GOODBYE, GOLDENEYE

Rag of black plastic, shred of a kite
caught on the telephone cable above the bay
has twisted in the wind all winter, summer, fall.

Leaves of birch and maple, brown paws of the oak
have all let go but this. Shiny black Mylar
on stem strong as fishline, the busted kite string

whipped around the wire and knotted—how long
will it cling there? Through another spring?
Long barge nudged up channel by a snorting tug,

its blunt front aproned with rot-black tires—
what is being hauled in slime-green drums?
The herring gulls that used to feed their young

on the shore—puffy, wide-beaked babies standing
spraddle-legged and crying—are not here this year.
Instead, steam shovel, bulldozer, cement mixer

rumble over sand, beginning the big new beach house.
There'll be a hotdog stand, flush toilets, trash—
plastic and glass, greasy cartons, crushed beercans,

barrels of garbage for water rats to pick through.
So, goodbye, goldeneye, and grebe and scaup and loon.
Goodbye, morning walks beside the tide tinkling

among clean pebbles, blue mussel shells and snail
shells that look like staring eyeballs. Goodbye,
kingfisher, little green, black crowned heron,

snowy egret. And, goodbye, oh faithful pair of
swans that used to glide—god and goddess
shapes of purity—over the wide water.

SUMMERFALL

After "the glorious Fourth," summer tumbles down.
An old hotel in Salt Lake City, Newhouse its name—
methodically installed with plugs of dynamite

for time-released explosion—burst!
Stupendously slow, the upper stories first. So
the whole west side of summer shears away.

Leafy cornices and balconies shatter, whirl down,
reduce to particles. The smash accelerates
as autumn's avalanches slide in planned relay,

until blanked out behind gray towers of fog.
All will be flattened. Graciousness, out of date,
must go, in instantaneous shock.

But Mind projects it slow,
stretching movement out, each flung chunk floating
awhile, weightless, and with no noise.

Mind reluctantly unbuilds summer.
The four-square, shade-roofed mansions
of an early, honest, work-proud era fall

to the dust of demolition. Prompt to come, ye Saints,
your condominiums, high-rise business, boosted
economy, new cash flow.

After "the rockets' red glare," here on the eastern shore
a sick acrylic sunset loiters in murky haze.
The sequence of such evenings will be speeding up.

FROM A DAYBOOK

January 29th
Black-white-black the flock of scaup
pushing hard against whittles of the tide.
Each seems to have a window in the side.
Light might shine right through. The day
is frozen gray, a steel engraving,
the bay a pewter plate, sky icy mist.
Black scaup, bluish bills poked forward,
float, white middles on dark water are
transparent squares of light.

February 10th
Snow beginning makes a brightening.
Scarce white fur released from gray sky
starts to gather, dense in darkening air.
Expectation freshens the hibernating mind.
Is the scene beyond the apron of the eye
about to shift? At dawn will new birds
arrive, stand vivid on an ermine floor?
Inside, we now vicarious watch
winter's rigid climax. Crystal by crystal
formed in the opening of mind's burrow,
the dream of death rehearsed, and the
costume fashioned. Of rich white fur
the curtain, parting, deepens its folds.

March 17th, Before Storm
Sky, a red-striped flag, billows
over cobalt tide. A low lightblade
snags on ridges of the waves.
Wind begins to agonize in bare trees
and it rips lengthwise the murky
banner. There is a clear green
naked staring iris between clouds.

May 28th

Ripe in the green leaves (a whistle
urgent and tireless) a pulse of pleasure
sits, shaped to fit my hand. Radish-
bright, it pretends to hide behind
the leaves. Instead revealed, is seen
vulnerable and flagrant. Radical
whistle, color ripe and candid, the pulse
of pleasure shaped to fit my hand,
has wings. Has wings. Has vanished.

July 3rd, Morning Descent

Gray wing divides blue from white.
Blue blank as swipe of waterpaint.
White unsmirched, mat without sketch.
Gray wing whisked by cold upper air.
Slantwise shadow brushes its tip.
The carriage rocks. Blue widens,
white brightens. Round-as-Rubens'
forms begin. To become shaded
on one side. They sedately shove
each other. Become each others'
bodies. Blank mat gray wing severs,
dives through, slides under, hides blue.
Depth becomes height. Wing downglides.
A long white slope. The carriage stops.

September 8th

So long I've wanted to get him
into my word-cage, Wildhead,
his call a pack of cards
shuffled, riffled, crisply
reshuffled. Then expertly

gathered up, he flies
beside the canal over the sandy
road and the bay. Blue and
white and belted, buoyant,
flamboyant acrobat, airclimber,
clown, hovering diver. Wildhead,
best of fishers, King!

October 24th
Tall sails going away, turn
from broadside to profile
in evening light. Their spiny
masts support great silken quills.
Wind loves feather, flag and sail.
Colored cloths lick out, feeling
for the panting wind. Gulls
hover the tall white pinion
shapes of ships going away.

November 15th
The horizon has disappeared.
A gigantic pair of shears
has cut it off. Or it was
effaced by a thick fog eraser.
Crossing the waves' border,
a faint boat starts to creep
the sky, keep vertical, sail
nudged by an odorless wind.

TWO

RAINBOW HUMMINGBIRD LAMPLIGHT

rain bow		bird light
humming bird	light humming	rain humming
lamp light	rain light	humming bow
	rain bird	

	rain bird	
rain light	humming bow	light humming
rain humming	lamp light	bird light
humming bird		rain bow

A shack of dark rainstreaked boards, steep pitched roof, smoke from the tin chimney pushing out into fog. On a mountain in California: high desert of chaparral, yucca, agave, juniper, manzanita, desert yew, prickly pear on the ridges and in the ravines. And, hanging from a rafter at the peak of the ceiling in the small square room, whose wide old stained knotholed boards let wind and rain through the splintery cracks, but which is furnished with a big black Huntsman's wood stove on which we can pop corn, boil coffee, fry steak if we have it, and that burns chunky split logs even when they are wet from the frequent rains, is a once-glittering glass prismed Mexican chandelier with a circle of sconces in which the heels of sooty yellow candles sit. We do not use it for light—there's no way to reach the candles to light or to snuff them. We use the graceful hourglass-shaped kerosene lamp—the thick curved glass base is bottom half of the hourglass—the chimney's outline is that of a seamstress' dress dummy of long ago.

When the sun shines on this rough little cabin, to which has been attached a somewhat larger newly built structure of cinderblock covered with adobe, and also furnished with a Huntsman's stove, making two studios that share a propaned pipelined kitchenette and bath between them—the cabin being the writer's half of what's called "The Writer/Painter House"—wonderful birds come to the round wood table on the raw-wood deck that hangs like a shelf over the slope of the north-facing mountain. The table is a large wirecable spool spread with peanut bits, cracked corn and sunflower seeds. To the feeding table come golden-crowned sparrow, brown towhee, rufous-sided towhee, scrub jay, for instance. And Bewick's wren will trill from a near clump of live oak, through which is trying to grow a young palo verde. And the curve-billed thrasher with icy eye will be mocking crisply from a branch of manzanita, and ravens will be sailing and remarking, while the redtailed hawk will be circling high above the mountain. There's a snowtopped view of Mt. San Gorgonio, looking a bit like Fujiyama, poking up behind the lower Black Hills and, opposite, to the southwest, the sinuous swells of the far pale Nameless Mountains. From our bed on this first morning, we saw, out the deck door, in the west the white-gold moon, full and almost transparent, setting above, and then behind, these mountains, at the same time as the sun, a big red shield, came up in the east throwing long salmon ribbon-streaks under the moon—which, seen through the flawed glass of the deck door, seemed to be square-edged and eight-sided, like a Susan B. Anthony dollar.

This place we've come to, a preserve for working artists and writers, is remote and wild. Last night coyotes bayed nearby in weird harmony. We discovered a rodent, large by the sound of its teeth—maybe a packrat—tearing at the adobe calking in a closed space between the rafters and the roof where the new part of the double studio was joined to the old. No bang of broomstick made it pause, but when the "boo-booboo" of the great horned owl, who roosts in the tallest yew upslope, began at about three a.m., the rat fell silent. After unpacking the van in the late afternoon, we had early supper outdoors seated on thick bench-wide wedges of the woodpile in the shade. It was still hot before the mountain wind that begins with sundown. We ate fresh grapefruit slices and halves of avocado squirted with lemon juice, pecans, coconut strips and a ripe papaya, while watching a pair of charcoal black lizards spill from a space between logs. Trickling along the ground, they suddenly stopped, one behind the other, petrified. Not another flick for five minutes. When we looked away for a second and then looked back, they were gone. We went exploring. Unexpectedly, half a mile up a corkscrew dirt road into foothills overlooking green valley ranches and cattle pastures, this nook of the wild where fang of

puma, talon of raven, Cooper's hawk, coyotes, rattlesnakes and bobcats may still be met, such tender life as exists in lily ponds also exists: shadowy fish hanging in the ooze and waving mosses, monarch butterflies and dragonflies, bestirring the air above the loose mosaic of flat yellow, brown and red pond lily leaves, squish-bodied frogs, darting tadpoles. Skipping the sandy natural paths among scrub oak and brittlebush were brown rabbits with white scuts, their round wall-eyes set far back in their soft heads, and we've been told small deer may come down from the higher hills before sunup, to sample the fruit of dewy prickly pear. Across the gulch, sharing the top twigs of a wrung-dry dead yucca with fierce thrasher and pushy jay—what a sweet surprise—was Anna's hummingbird. Only a bit bigger than a bumblebee, her short hooks of feet gripping tight, her long probe at an arrogant angle, her pulsing throat, brilliant green when her head turns left, crimson when it swivels right, she was sounding her whisper-like signal as she sucked gnats out of their gossamer twirls in slanting sunlight. Now, from the top of an upright post at one corner of the deck of our shack and cabin, we've hung a slender cruet of red glass and filled it with sugar water which the Anna's can sip from a little cock at the base. Tiny helicopters, wings whirring that hold them poised in air, the hummingbirds are taking turns zooming in to feed right above our breakfast bowls, as we begin our first full day here in the high desert. Our bowls hold the biggest juiciest strawberries in California. We get them from the outdoor fruit market, or can pick for ourselves, if we like, in the valley below.
What's that, moving molasses-slow
over rock-strewn sand down there,
through the enigmatic glare
of sun in the gully under our deck—
mica-speckled, white, gray and black
as the sand it crosses? It's the Diamond Back
who now glides back
to his cool denhole in—see?—
that boulder's crack
between brittlebush and Joshua tree.

MORNING AT POINT DUME

Blond stones all round-sided,
that the tide has tumbled on sand's table,
like large warm loaves strewn in the sun.

Wet pathways drain among them, sandgrains
diamond in morning light.
A high-hipped dog trots toward the sea,

followed by a girl, naked, young,
breasts jouncing, and long fair hair.
Girl and dog in the hissing surf

roister, dive and swim together,
bodies flashing dolphin-smooth,
the hair in her delta crisp dark gold.

The Pacific is cold. Rushed ashore on a wave,
her body blushes with stings of spume.
Running upslope, the circling dog

leaps to her hand, scatters spray
from his thick blond malamute fur.
Together they twine the stone loaves' maze.

Girl lets her glistening belly down
on a yellow towel on hard hot sand,
dog panting, *couchant* by her side.

Five surfers in skintight black
rubber suits, their plexiglass
boards on shoulders, stride the shore,

their eyes searching the lustrous water
for the hills of combers that build far out,
to mount and ride the curling snowtops.

The sunburned boys in phalanx pass,
squinting ahead, scuffing sand.
Without a glance at the yellow towel

they advance to the sea.
Enormous breakers thunder in.
Falling, they shake the ground.

A DAY LIKE ROUSSEAU'S *DREAM*

Paradise lasts for a day. Crowns of the palms lift
and glisten, their hairy trunks breathe with the sway
of fronds in striped light. Balconies of leaves
mount in layers to lunettes of sky. The ground is
stippled by shadows of birds. In a blink, they flit
into hiding, each disguised against its own color
in the tall leafwall that pockets a thousand nests
and husks, cones, seedpods, berries, blossoms.

Look closely. The whites of creature eyes shift
like diamonds of rain. Flowers are shrieks of color
in the gullies, are shaped to leap or fly, some with
sharp orange beaks or curved purple necks, or they
thrust out vermilion tongues. Velvet clubs, jeweled
whips, silky whisks and puffs and beaded clusters
combine their freakish perfumes.

Beside a slow gray stream, lilies, startling white,
unfurl like crisp breastpocket handkerchiefs.
Hummingbirds upright in flight flash sequined throats.
Eyes of an owl, goldrimmed circles, dilate, then shut
where he stands on a strut in the moiré of a datepalm
umbrella. Smooth trunks of eucalyptus twist up into
sunlight where, on a dangling basketnest, the hooded
oriole swings, ripe apricot.

High on a barkpeeled limb, is that a redhaired gibbon
hanging by one arm? And, drooping from a vine,
a boa's muscular neck, lidless eye and scimitar smile?
Are sagbellied panthers, partly eclipsed in bamboo shade

gliding behind that thicket? Is there a pygmy,
silver-eyed, black as the cabinet of shadow he hides in,
wearing a cockatoo on top of his ashen frizz?

Paradise lasts for a day. Be seated, with legs akimbo,
central on a mat of moss. Focus and penetrate the long
perspective between the palisades of green. Stabbing
through slits of light, your eyes may find—
couched in fern in a sunny alcove, melonpink body and
blackflagged head, eggshell-eyed, scarlet-lipped—
that magnetic, ample, jungle odalisque.

The eyes of animals enlarge to watch her, as all wind
drains from the leaves, and pure white scuts of clouds
appear in the zenith. Your gaze speeds to target,
the point of the V's black brush, where an oval
crack of space, a pod of white unpainted canvas, splits
for your eye's escape where her thighs do not touch.

SAGUAROS ABOVE TUCSON

Saguaros, fuzzy and huggable, greet us, seeming to stream
down the Rincon foothills as the car climbs. Their plump
arms branch, bend upward, enthused. Each prickly person,
droll, gregarious, we would embrace, but, up close, rigid
as cast plaster, spikey, bristling—how dare we touch?
Among the palo verde, teddybear cholla, ocotillo,
bristlebush and organpipe, we meet the desert tribe,
our friends from last year, standing in place, saluting

with their many arms. Granddaddies have most, are tallest
and toughest. Great girths they display, with numerous
bulging offspring graft-on-graft attached.
Adolescents, green and comical, big cucumbers, boast only
beginning bulbs of arms. A few peculiars, single, slim,
the air private around them, stand lonely, limbless—
perhaps forever young?— Low on the ground, babies,
fat little barrels, have only heads as yet, and sprout

scarce blond quills. We'd like to stop the car, get out
and climb the flinty gullies, walk to meet these giant
innocents, our friends, say Howdy, hug, take all their
stuckout hands. But, ouch! We do not know their ritual
handshake, or how to make retract their dangerous nails.
In spring, their heads were crowns of bloom, dainty and
festive. Flowers come out of their ears, out of fingers
and elbows come rainfresh colors, buds like blushing fruits.

Finches fix themselves in rings around the thorny brows,
whistling from rosy throats. Why are the little birds
not pierced? How do they perch so carelessly on
peaks of prickly needle-twigs?

When from freezing, lightning, windthrow or old age,
in a hundred and fifty years or more, the giants die,
they still stand. Shriveled, blackened, dried and peeling
scabby corpses, tall untouchables, they haunt the hills.

And elf owls roost in the breasts of the dead saguaros.
One moonless night last year we discovered them with
a flashlight. In a chardark hole at vestpocket height
in the ghost of an old saguaro we found round yellow eyes
crossed and weird: a tiny pale-streaked owl hunched
in a pulpy torso whose broken twists of arms, long fallen,
lay around it on the ground.
We looked for more. Still, as if stuffed, the owls stared,

framed in the cameos of our hypnotic beams aimed
at the hollow chests of the dead saguaros.
On sunny mornings this year, Rivoli's hummingbirds
will hover and snick, ignite and gyrate in their courting
dives above the tall, tough, corduroy bodies and
blooming heads of sturdy young saguaros. Again astonished,
we'll ask each other: On such stiletto-pointed pates
how is it that the elf owl mates?

ECLIPSE MORNING

Black sleet, bituminous flecks
disfigure that face. Stigmata
make it the more mysterious this
morning, the sun to be lidded
by moon's shadow.
Midnight's inkblot to be spilled,
sun's face filled, dilated to
a blind iris, the huge splash
of light blackened.
A greenish scrim lowers over
everything a powder like soot.
Moon slides between the plate of
great light and earth.
The dark dot is cast.
A startled woodthrush begins its
twilight ee-o-lay. A roused owl
erects its ears, stares, prepares
to hunt. Flowers that dawn has
just opened obey the signal to
close. At climax, a spree of wind
chills every leaf. Lawn pricks up
each blade, silver as with frost.
Three medallions, sun, moon, earth,
are strung on one thread.
Gorgon's head is lopped, the image
struck from the flashing shield.
And we, who open and close to our
sun's smile, or to its glare of
rage, for one astounding moment
see it quenched. In the blind
planetarium of the mind flickers
that face of feathered fire,
the cheek birthmarked with spots.

THE CROSS SPIDER

The 1st Night
      A spider, put outside the world,
given the Hole of Space for her design,
herself a hub all hollow, having no weight,
tumbled counterclockwise, paralytically slow
into the Coalsack.
Free where no wind was, no floor, or wall,
afloat eccentric on immaculate black,
she tossed a strand straight as light,
hoping to snag on perihelion and invent
the Edge, the Corner and the Knot.
In an orbit's turn, in glint and floss
of the crossbeam, Arabella caught
the first extraterrestrial Fly
of Thought. She ate it, and the web.

The 2nd Night
      "Act as if no center exists,"
Arabella advised herself. Thus inverted
was deformed the labyrinth of grammar.
Angles melted, circles unravelled, ladders
lost their rungs and nothing clinched.
At which the pattern of chaos became plain.
She found on the second night her vertigo
so jelled she used it for a nail
to hang the first strand on.
Falling without let, and neither up nor down,
how could she fail?
No possible rim, no opposable middle,
geometry as yet unborn, as many nodes and navels

as wishes—or as few—could be spun.
Falling began the crazy web.
Dizziness completed it. A half-made, half-mad
asymmetric unnameable jumble, the New
became the Wen. On Witch it sit wirligiggly.
No other thing or Fly alive.
Afloat in the Black Whole, Arabella
crumple-died. Experiment frittered.

An experiment conducted in Skylab 2 in orbit around
Earth in 1973 was to watch a cross spider, *Araneida dia-
dema*, spin a web in space.

SHUTTLES

ONE
April 12, 1981

FLASH! SHOCK! BLAST! "Looks like a statue going up,"
Dan Rather says. Hoisted on a widening, roaring ramp
of flame and cloud, it sizzles aloft. On the ground,
a former astronaut says, "I feel lev-i-ta-ted!"
A pair of local bald eagles scream, "Roger, we copy,
Roger, we copy." Already out of this world, and Go
for orbit, the two-man crew hang vertical in their straps,
snug as twin kangaroos in Mommy's pouch. Boosted into
the loop, escaped from gravity, they'll glide upside down
and backwards—"upside down with the tail poked forward,"
as Rather says. But blood in their veins won't know it.
The blindness of space won't show it.

While still on the pad at Canaveral, stuck to the belly
of the giant booster, flanked by tall cylinders of solid
fuel, the blunt, black-nosed little plane, with its cockpit
window-eyes and white stubby wings back-canted: "Looks
like a folded fly," I say, seeing only the blurry TV visual,
black and white. For Columbia's first flight, I was far
from home. To zip this fly at 16,000 miles per hour
to orbit cost 14 billion bucks. "Apollo was only a star-
ship. The Shuttle is a truck," the tech experts brag.
Sons of Columbia will survey the ring road of our planet
to acquire squat-room on the new frontier. "We need pit-
stops and body shops deployed, to equip the star wars
of the future."

All systems are Go . . . . . . And now, 36 orbits and 54 hours
later, all systems are Come, for landing at Edwards in the

Mojave Desert. Rightside up, Columbia and crew face home,
nose pitched up sharp, for the descent. At 18 times
the speed of sound, the stub-winged fly drops and pierces
through Earth's atmosphere. Temperature leaps in the crew
and in their craft. The pilot's arms grow heavy as anvils.
Stress of re-entry piles weight on weight, and hearts and
temples pound. From Euphoria of space, from the smooth
angelic float, the grab of gravity is a jagged, hot rebirth.

All systems are Come. Columbia, the glider, blunt little fly,
weight 2 million pounds, size of a DC-9, pulls down in S-curves
out of the sky. In the grainy air of earth, she tends to
wobble at first, roll and yaw. But the dry lakebed of Edwards
is in sight. At 10,000 feet, at a 20-degree angle, losing
200 feet per second, at 290 knots, she drops. Banking, she
lines up with the runway, flares in at a descent rate of 50
feet per second, on stubby Delta wings, makes a graceful
drive-test-U, and skateboards the runway, spurting a wake of
desert sand. She stops neatly athwart the target, giant X,
which is the computer team's exact demand.

TWO
November 12, 1981

"We have LIFT-OFF!" A jolt like earthquake, then
the jubilant scream-gush-roar. From its trench
of flame an elongated Taj Mahal jumps upward,
straddling its wide boiling plume of smoke and
spitting rectal fire.

Scrubbed last week, but launched 10:10 a.m. today,
Columbia soars toward orbit. The roll maneuver
is smoothly made. Now, far and steep
into Florida blue, blurts and pulses the red
explosion.

Telephoto and Television frames contain it
in vivid Trinitron. Twin flanking rocket boosters
fall away, "each a bit shorter," Dan Rather says,
"than the Statue of Liberty." The huge external
fuel tank with three engines

(meaning the tall white central tower of the Taj,
on whose back Columbia rides until separation)
"releases as much energy as 23 Hoover Dams," Dan says.
That craft and its crew got back intact, too,
after four days, some glitches—a few—

after the tests for handling payloads: "O.K., Joe,
it's a great day for the Ace Moving Co.," said
the capsule communicator, alluding to the ultimate
purpose, which is "eventually to operate a fleet
of orbital freighters."

When all three wheeels ease down
in a desert mirage, and the pilots
in gold jumpsuits emerge, at 5:05 p.m.
in a blizzard of sand, wild cheers
go up from the throng. A graceful touchdown.

FOUR (I missed the Third)
June 17, 1982

"We've cleared the tower!" Again. And again we'll clear.
"Oh God! My God!" is the groan that hiccoughs forth,
as bulbous clots of smoke, a whoosh of flame
pushes the THING gigantic up again.

The ground bounces, the sonic shock begets a booming chasm
of echoes. It seems enough to shatter granite.
The TV screen crazes under the blast. The hands
of a thousand cameras go spastic, lenses crack.

Do not eardrums snap, eyeballs collapse, lungs inflate
to bursting? The two in the cockpit, couched and strapped,
need just seconds to survive the slam of sound,
the flattening of their guts. Then the boosters

peel away, and tumble. Only minutes until the tall tank
slices off and falls, a gray slug, into the sea.
Again it's Go for orbit. It makes the first pass
over Africa's west bulge that used to nuzzle

the continental hollow of South America when Earth was young.
Columbia for the fourth time pushes its THING
on the way to its sling 150 miles above Earth, to circle
eight days this time, until Independence Day,

leaving below the heavy ring of sludge, its poison,
great gouts and smudges of choking cloud, to join the other
missile garbage of the air—(over 2,500 satellites there
already)—to spoil the weather, ruin human atmosphere.

We will equip (and expose) ourselves in space,
the High Frontier, half of Earth showing the other half
who's biggest, stiffest, most macho, who can
get it UP, can get it OFF, the quickest.

TOO BIG FOR WORDS
January 26, 1986

11:38 a.m., Launch Pad 39B, 25th Shuttle Mission: "We have
lift-off! . . . It has cleared the tower!"

Challenger, rolling on its back, loops out over ocean,
soaring at 1,538 miles per hour, 4.9 miles high,
two side-boosters packing solid propellant, the main
central booster burning 526,000 gallons of liquid oxygen
and hydrogen . . . fuel of the sun, the stars.

About to punch through the sound barrier at 1,977 MPH,
three times the speed of sound, 10.4 miles high:
Mission Control: "Challenger, go throttle up!"
Commander: "Roger. Go throttle up."

SEARING BRIGHT BALL OF LIGHT. A shuddering roar . . .

Mission Control (mechanical voice): "We're one minute, 15
seconds velocity, 2,900 feet per second, altitude 9 nautical
miles, range distance 7 nautical miles . . ."

Not true. Challenger, engulfed in flames, does not exist.

The 122-foot orbiter in blazing chunks, for 45 minutes
rains down onto the Atlantic, 18 miles northeast of
Canaveral. Ships and helicopters, a squad of over 1,000
people rushing to the impact area, cannot get within range,
either by air or water, because of falling debris.

FIREBALL. THE SHUDDERING ROAR. Then, blank silence.
From a bloating ram's head of white cloud, enormous horns
uncurl, inflate on blue. The searing rocket boosters
spiral free. The two-story cabin with the crew
breaks out of the nose cone, falls nine miles to the sea.

Built for orbit, Challenger seated seven human bodies.
Incinerated? Cremated? Poisoned by fumes? Suffocated
by loss of pressure? Slammed dead on impact with the sea?

Blizzard of debris. Pieces too small, too many, ever to
put together. Event too big for words . . . For the next
week the most-played lottery number in Florida was 1138.

Never to be erased, that white burst inflates, inflates,
inflates perpetual, on the sky of mind.

One morning, on the beach near Canaveral, a navy blue sock
washed up. In it, a fragment of bone and human tissue.
Evidence without connection . . .

Item in the news in April: Computer-enhanced films show
the cabin, tiny thimble, tumbling intact toward ocean.
"It really shook me to watch that film," said the source
at NASA. "It turned in tumbling. It caught the sun.
You could see the rate of spin."

By July NASA conceded that the crew, at "Go throttle up!"
had to have known the lift-off was fatal. Recorded by
the "black box" finally recovered from Challenger's debris,
Commander's voice was heard: He said, "Uh-oh." It took
ten seconds to hit water. *They were alive. They knew.*

COMET WATCH
ON INDIAN KEY

Night of April 10, 1986

Bright splendid head of
Halley's Comet . . . Comet
coming. Coming again.
Not seen since May 8, 1910.
Called Dirty Snowball, and
Finger of God Pointing,
and Plunger to Disaster . . .
Dis-aster means bad star.
Comet coming. Coming again,
elliptically swishing out
from behind the far
blind side of Sun. Gaseous
Dustball, probably lumpy,
it lets nest, in its
diaphanous tail thinned by
the Solar Wind, Aldebaran
and Betelgeuse undimmed.
Comet coming coming again.
Wonder of wonders . . . Who
will be on watch on that
spring night in 2062?

AHNIGHITO

Enormous beast on six legs stands in the Hall
of Meteorites. Small children like to crouch
or crawl beneath him. Looking up, they feel
he's friendly. True, he can't attack. Cold,
dense, heavier than iron, his ridged back shows
scalloped melt-marks. Flaming lump, he tumbled,

blunt buffalo-head, imbedded in a self-dug
blasthole, congealed in earth for centuries.
Reptilian his look of never-needing-to-move.
You can't see him breathe. But the space about
his outline vibrates. Power like dust of mica
seems to swirl around his bulk.

Six chrome poles the paraplegic monster's
mounted on. The children stoop around those
legs, rumpus under the heavy belly, lay their
petal cheeks against harsh metal, and listen
for what might snort within. They pet and pat
the face that, here or there, might show an eye

or nostril about to bloom, or short thick
warted horn. Half his snout, distended like
a dragon's, has been filed flat, rubbed bright
as nickel, slick to stroking hands. This patch
of the beast's shag peeled, planed and flashing,
has worn out many tools.

Howling fire fattened to a roar when he fell,
fragment of a star, or lava Minotaur, gnarled
hide charred black, great clinker bounding
down from the fiery shore of Universe. Beast
not of this earth, beneath which children play
as Romulus and Remus trustfully suckled.

IF I HAD CHILDREN

If I had children, I might name
them astrometeorological names:
Meridian, a girl. Zenith, a boy.
Eclipse, a pretty name for either one.
Anaximander, ancient Greek scientist
(who built a gnomon on Lacedaemon,
and with it predicted the exact date

that city would be destroyed by
earthquake).... Anaximander, wonderful
name for a girl. Anny could be her
nickname. Ion, short for ionosphere,
would make a graceful name for
a boy. Twins could be named after
planets: Venus and Mercury, or

Neptune and Mars. They'd adore each
other's heavenly bodies shining
upon their doubles on Earth.
And have you ever thought that, of
the Nine, only one planet is female?
Venus. Unless Earth is. So, seven
of Sun's children, it seems, are male.

But, if I had children, and grandchild-
ren, then greatgrandchildren, myriads
of newborn moons and moonlets crowding
into the viewfinder would furnish me
names both handsome and sweet:
Phoebe, Rhea, Dione among daughters
of Saturn, with Titan and Janus the

brothers. Io, Ganymede and Callisto,
Jupiter's boys: Europa and little
Amalthea, their sisters.
On Io, most exotic of the Galilean
moons, are mapped six great-and-grand
volcanoes: Loki, Hemo, Horus, Daedalus,
Tarsis, Ra. Beauties all! But all

boys. Well, if I had children
I wouldn't fix genders or orbits, only
names for them. Wobbling Phobus,
distant child of Mars, misshapen as
a frozen potato. . . . If I had such a
lopsided moon, the name Phobus would
fit. And I'd love it just the same.

THREE

COME IN   GO OUT

A world of storm	A life of waves
Raging circles form	Tides and icy caves
Wind loops the globe	Sun scorching palms
Blizzards in the brain	Or deadening calms
Then modifying hope	A single summer day
A hoisted sail	Unfolds twinkling
On the dream trail	Flinches past the eye
Hummingbird's green	Bullet of gauze
Illuminant	Of primal cause

IN THE BODIES OF WORDS

For Elizabeth Bishop (1911–1979)

Tips of the reeds silver in sunlight. A cold wind
sways them, it hisses through quills of the pines.
Sky is clearest blue because so cold. Birds drop down
in the dappled yard: white breast of nuthatch, slate
catbird, cardinal the color of blood.

Until today in Delaware, Elizabeth, I didn't know
you died in Boston a week ago. How can it be
you went from the world without my knowing?
Your body turned to ash before I knew. Why was there
no tremor of the ground or air? No lightning flick
between our nerves? How can I believe? How grieve?

I walk the shore. Scraped hard as a floor by wind.
Screams of terns. Smash of heavy waves. Wind rips
the corners of my eyes. Salty streams freeze on my face.
A life is little as a dropped feather. Or split shell
tossed ashore, lost under sand. . . . But vision lives!
Vision, potent, regenerative, lives in bodies of words.
Your vision lives, Elizabeth, your words
from lip to lip perpetuated.

Two days have passed. Enough time, I think, for death
to be over. As if your death were not *before* my knowing.
For a moment I jump back to when all was well and ordinary.
Today I could phone to Boston, say Hello. . . . Oh, no!
Time's tape runs forward only. There is no replay.

Light hurts. Yet the sky is dull today. I walk the shore.
I meet a red retriever, young, eager, galloping
out of the surf. At first I do not notice his impairment.
His right hind leg is missing. Omens. . . .

I thought I saw a rabbit in the yard this morning.
It was a squirrel, its tail torn off. Distortions....

Ocean is gray again today, old and creased aluminum
without sheen. Nothing to see on that expanse.
Except, far out, low over sluggish waves, a long
clotted black string of cormorants trails south.
Fog-gray rags of foam swell in scallops up the beach,
their outlines traced by a troupe of pipers—
your pipers, Elizabeth!—their racing legs like spokes
of tiny wire wheels.

Faintly the flying string can still be seen.
It swerves, lowers, touching the farthest tips of waves.
Now it veers, appears to shorten, points straight out.
It slips behind the horizon. Vanished.

But vision lives, Elizabeth. Your vision multiplies,
is magnified in the bodies of words.
Not vanished, your vision lives from eye to eye,
your words from lip to lip perpetuated.

Bethany, Delaware
October 13–15, 1979

HER EARLY WORK

Talked to cats and dogs,
to trees, and to strangers.
To one loved, talked through
layers of masks.
To this day we can't know
who was addressed,
or ever undressed.
Because of the wraparounds,
overlaps and gauzes,
kept between words and skin,
we notice nakedness.
Wild and heathen scents
of shame or sin
hovered since childhood,
when the delicious was always
forbidden. "A Word With You"
had to be whispered,
spoken at the zoo,
not to be overheard
by eavesdropping ape or cockatoo.

ANGELS, EAGLES

Angels, eagles, owls among the heads
grafted on human shoulders, bronze
the dark of beachtree leaves, obscurely
shining. Ripple of ribs, tight hips
and thighs about to stride into flight.
And some have wings, elbows like wing-
joints, fingers becoming feathers.

Under a skylight on a low platform
Jacob hugs his angel. The struggle is
over, the match is tied, and strength
no longer virtue. Like boxers leaning
into the clinch, combat has left them
healthy, priapic, spent, and tender.
No referee arrives to split them.

Angel's curly head butts softly the
pectoral hollow of Jacob's shoulder
whose arm crosses the wingéd back,
one loose-balled fist resting on
Angel's neck. Nearby, beneath an arch:
grim heads of buzzards and of bats
trussed into sacks of their own skins.

Inchoate forms on taloned feet in static
decomposure, their jaws are open to moan
or screech. Raptors' profiles, cruel
and beautiful, erupt out of young boys'
torsos. A dead leather-look, iguana-
like, of sleepers on slabs on the floor
with legs, arms, heads, hollow bellies,
buttocks fused as in a common grave.

But horror is not evoked. Rather, grace,
proportion, the exquisite languor of
surrender. In a doorway leans a youth
with the head of a cat. The narrowed
eyes stare at the viewer through pupils
of green onyx, and tiny teeth smile
white in the cleft of the upper lip.

And look: in an inner nook in mellow
light, a woman's head on slender neck
is attached to a body ambiguous, while
the profile of marble wears the queendom
of a swan. This, the brightest head of
all the company grown from a black-as-
lava, probably male, form, is a radiant

shock. At which most strollers turn
aside. Toward which a few, like me,
like you, magnetically move. Something
human shows in every beast, and animal
beauty in human. Enigma reigns in the
room where bodies, more than human,

are more than merely alive. Yet all are
metal, and dead. And the sculptor
has been forgotten. Shadow without body,
he slips mind's view. Until we walk out
of the gallery onto the city street. Now
we remember him, *in his flesh*, walking,
as we walk among people. Forms he made

and makes, caressing and cursing, stretching again and again toward flight, toward
the immortal, these bodies of beast and
youth, demon and hero, predator, angel,
androgyne, chimaera, god, he engenders
with power, and marks each face and head
with his own ferocious beauty.

—*Homage to Leonard Baskin*

THE ELECT

Under the splendid chandeliers
the august heads are almost all
fragile, gray, white-haired or bald
against the backs of thronelike chairs.

They meet in formal membership
to pick successors to their seats,
having eaten the funeral meats,
toasted the names on the brass strips

affixed behind them, tier on tier,
on chairs like upright coffin tops.
When a withered old head drops,
up is boosted a younger's career.

The chamber is ancient and elite,
its lamps pour down a laureate gold.
Beyond the windows blue and cold
winter twilight stains the street,

as up from the river the wind blows
over slabs of a steep graveyard,
the names under snow. A last award:
to be elected one of those.

SHIFT OF SCENE AT GRANDSTAND

Fall, winter and spring on the same spread at Grandstand.
Last winter's ragged leaves poke through a flat

of melting snow. Exposed in the dun mat of the meadow,
holes of field mice and woodchuck show the scene

is being struck. From stiff, split creases, shuttles
of milkweed let their fleeces out. We see red-capped

spicules in the hoary moss. "British soldiers," Jane
says. Leslie picks a tiny dried-up sort of thimble

he names "St. James Wort." Other trinkets of fall
are strewn about: by the brook a bead-like ball, and

we find more of them, golden on the ice crust. I say,
"They're deer droppings. How neat!" Some props remain

from the act of winter: the elm's arterial system sprawls
against a cold, bare sky. Few buds are out, but spry

chickadees alight, matching the pussywillow's plush.
One bush wears a pale yellow veil in the hollow

where male kinglets flash rubies on their napes.
Red-vested robins and pink-billed juncos streak by,

stippling the new backdrop of the year. One blue jay
sounds his flute note to say that the curtain is about

to part on Groundhog making his second entrance. Now,
taking her cue for an extended dance, spangle-skirted

Rain arrives. Next, the main character, Lord Sun,
comes downstage. Scene I: Violets. Scene II: Greensward.

After which, a sudden switch to Scene III: Summer
from now on, by demand, booked to play at Grandstand.

LITTLE LION FACE

Little lion face
I stooped to pick
among the mass of thick
succulent blooms, the twice

streaked flanges of your silk
sunwheel relaxed in wide
dilation, I brought inside,
placed in a vase. Milk

of your shaggy stem
sticky on my fingers, and
your barbs hooked to my hand,
sudden stings from them

were sweet. Now I'm bold
to touch your swollen neck,
put careful lips to slick
petals, snuff up gold

pollen in your navel cup.
Still fresh before night
I leave you, dawn's appetite
to renew our glide and suck.

An hour ahead of sun
I come to find you. You're
twisted shut as a burr,
neck drooped unconscious,

an inert, limp bundle,
a furled cocoon, your
sun-streaked aureole
eclipsed and dun.

Strange feral flower asleep
with flame-ruff wilted ,
all magic halted,
a drink I pour, steep

in the glass for your
undulant stem to suck.
Oh, lift your young neck,
open and expand to your

lover, hot light.
Gold corona, widen to sky.
I hold you lion in my eye
sunup until night.

PALE SUN

Pallor of the December sun.
Far and small, on a plane
of water, sails point in three
directions, separate from
each other. One a white cutlass

tall in the low light. And two
squat triangles, blue and yellow.
The weather's strange,
like spring. The water's flat
as a tin floor. A single

song sparrow sounds a note,
but can't be seen—gray in a gray
bush by the path on the sloped
shore. I lean there
against a thick boulder.

Warm light strokes my face.
I see in my mind my face,
flaccid, mournful, old. Well
it will be older. A slim boy
walks by, with a gliding gait.

His shadow crosses mine
on the path. From a strap
on his shoulder hangs a leather
case. What's in it? A weapon?
The three sails, coming about,

enlarge, converging toward
the jetty. Slaps and plops
of the languid tide barely heard;
instead I hear a clear
delicate run of reedy notes.

Walking back around the point
I see the boy seated on a bulkhead,
leather case open beside him,
face raised to the sun.
He's playing his flute.

A NEW PAIR

Like stiff whipped cream in peaks and tufts afloat,
the two on barely gliding waves approach.

One's neck curves back, the whole head to the eyebrows
hides in the wing's whiteness.

The other drifts erect, one dark splayed foot
lifted along a snowy hull.

On thin, transparent platforms of the waves
the pair approach each other, as if without intent.

Do they touch? Does it only seem so to my eyes'
perspective where I stand on shore?

I wish them together, to become one fleece enfolded, proud
vessel of cloud, shape until now unknown.

Tense, I stare and wait, while slow waves carry them
closer. And side does graze creamy side.

One tall neck dips, is laid along the other's back,
at the place where an arm would embrace.

A brief caress. Then both sinuous necks arise,
their paddle feet fall to water. As I stare,
with independent purpose at full sail, they steer apart.

SOME QUADRANGLES

The 1982 Harvard Phi Beta Kappa Poem

On a vast magic carpet the students squat,
legs akimbo, in loose clumps of three or four
reading *The Wildcat*, hunched over large cups
of ice and cola. The grass worn down to dirt
in patches, its nap gray from incessant sun,
if dried dogshit leaves a smudge on faded jeans,
no sweat, it's just another dust unnoticed.
January. But Arizona time's tattoo extends eternal.
On another part of the quad, outstretched asleep,
male torsos redden to Indian, chest hairs bleach.
Free of skirts and scuffs, girls' bare legs
jackknife or V-spread, blond and carrot hairs
snag light, as does the fuzz on cholla and dearhorn.
Around the quad, trunks of palms, thick-middled
Doric, belted with shag beneath splayed crowns
leave archways for the sun's wide klieg.
Bookbags make good cushions or, rather, blocks
for under necks. Maybe studies are done
under sunwarm eyelids by the brain's left half
turned low, while the right simmers to a sensual
disco beat. Does the carpet undulate? It seems
to float somnambulistically just off the ground—
although it *is* the ground—while above it,
wingtip to wingtip on high blank blue,
mechanical vultures climb in pairs aslant
from out of Monthan Air Force Base to the south.
Lower, sluggish, a mud-gray shark, a widebody,
horizontally crosses sky in the other direction.
Followed by a brace of graceful jets,
slim aluminum swans in a silent glide.
When they are dots on distance their huge noise
arrives, horrendous. The campus is not disturbed.

Pleasant torpor here on the shabby precious grass,
where a mass of young bodies in languid
enchanted tableaux—figures on the carpet—
have the far jagged Rincons for a frame.

In snowy compounds of the north and east,
the noonhour over, two hours ago at least,
the freezing quads are almost empty,
belong to the wind. They are white and lonely.
It is indoors, on hallway carpets and in
libraries' pillowy chairs and divans,
the students crouch or sleep. They live in
their ski coats, snooze in their boots.
If unlucky enough to get only table or desk
in study hall, they sink heads on bookbags,
dreaming heads, with lots and lots of hair.
Hair is piled and spilled among books
on the tables—dark hair bushy or kinky.
Bridges of sideburns join the beards on boys.
On girls, big hats of hair, and comfy hoods
of foaming curls help them endure the Buffalo
and Minneapolis winters. In lamplight
on the stairs, in corridors, and in the lounges,
like woolly sheep huddled against the blizzard,
they browse, preferring to keep close to ground.
Some, parked on their bellies by the radiators,
look like toboggans or sleds.

In April, in St. Louis, in a rare warm week,
dark grass of the Common already thick,
a few daffodils out that the wind whips
along the borders of buildings. In a boxlike space

between stone walls with towers like a castle,
spreads the carpet in the stingy sun. Not bared
to the sun—too chilly for that—but, as elsewhere,
close together the students cuddle on the ground.
No matter turf's still wet, mud showing through.
In wool plaids, parkas, and the sturdy indigo Levis
favored in the Midwest, they warm hands around
paper mugs of coffee, pizza pie in cardboard flats
balanced on folded knees. The Buddha position.
Somehow now that's how you sit if you're in college.

Is it so in Harvard Yard? On your historic
greens, between the bells, do students squat
or lie flat out, in spots of sun and shade,
snacking and reading *The Crimson*?

At, for instance, *my* college (which was Utah
State Agricultural at that time, long, long ago)
the students were *upright*. Yes, we comported
ourselves with *respect* for the institution and
the *privilege* vouchsafed us. (I do not think
I've ever said that word out loud before.) We
had goals. And we climbed. We climbed the hill,
a foothill of the canyon, the same we used
for sleighing when it snowed. We huffed and
puffed under sonorous bongs from the belltower
whose carpentered peak was a big inspiring "A."
"Develops calves and lungs," Dad used to say.
"Prepares you for effort. The physical sparks
the mental climb." Well, maybe. Few students
had cars then. Yamahas hadn't happened, and
our campus was too steep for bikes.

Now, of course, it's bigger and modernized.
Expanded by the bulldozers, it spreads on,
up the canyon benches. There's a maze (a mess)
of approaches to cement parking lots, densely
planted with metal *Restricted* signs. But Old Main
remains, and much of the green which is framed
by ancient giant spruce and pine. There is
still space. Space remains in the West.
We were farmers' or cattlemen's kids, expected
to dress and behave in accord with our luck
at being in college. Of course we didn't
wear Levis. They were for milking cows.
There was no such thing as a student *lounge*.
The library was straight chairs around long,
thick, lamp-shaded, oakgrained tables.
Attention, Attendance, and proper Attire
were seldom challenged. We competed—check this!—
we competed to be good. Most of us did. How
dull! But that's what was *hep*, long before
that word made the dictionary. "Good student"
didn't mean brilliant scholar, original mind,
or even eagerness to learn. It meant programmed
to please—not so much our teachers, but mainly
our peers. Our goal was to fit the mold that
seemed assigned by those around us. We used
our quad of perfectly barbered grass only for
crossing from class to class. And we walked
on the crosswalks while walking and crossing.
Naturally, no foot should be set on the carpet.
Might wear it out! I do remember how it smelled
heavenly on dewy mornings after a mowing,
which sometimes left unlopped the subversive heads

of a dandelion or two. . . . Girls' heads—
(yes, we said "girls" not "women" then)—
were marcelled. Men were clean-shaven. Decent,
earnest, orderly, ambitious, we climbed up
College Hill, to join conformity, the majority
at the top. Notice how, seen in the pool of time,
present and past reflect each other—upside down!

Shall I talk of Texas, Pennsylvania, Idaho?
Or North Carolina, where the mockingbirds sing Soul,
copied from miniature Sonys the students wear
while jogging? Or of Washington Square, Manhattan's
grungy downtown campus, where drunks drink,
pushers push, pigeons shit on the benches, and,
nonetheless, blissful babies sleep in carriages
in the safer section, where pairs of old men on SS,
at cement tables hover over large, ancient, wooden
Hungarian chessmen. One day I heard one guffaw,
asking the other: "What should I do, now I'm retired?
Put on my leisure suit and take a tour in my RV?"
There used to be grass in Washington Square.
That carpet is worn out. But not the storied
magic. It's there.

On Southern California campuses the Angels walk
beneath peartree blooms, past hibiscus hedges
and waterlily ponds—beautiful male and female
thighs, in cutoffs, feet in sandals, chests bared,
those in T-shirts, unbra-ed. The tall, the tanned
bright-haired stroll to class, or they go
on skateboards or on bikes. And they bring their dogs.
Unleashed, luxurious breeds convene on the quads,

to chase, wrestle, and mount each other.
They wade in the fountains, race to capture
Frisbees tossed. At lunch hour, which can be
all hours from eleven to four, marmoreal poses
are taken on the plushy green. The quad's
a sculpture court. Spaced out, laid back, mellow,
buns to the ground, the Angels lounge, reading
The Bruin (sort of) and lapping ice-cream cones.
Any dog lays belly to grass, lifts ass, gets a lick.

For a very long time now, it seems, it's been trendy
to hang loose, slouch, be scruffy, drop out, turn on.
I guess it started with *Howl*, got a solid shove from
Hair. Quite early the neat Beatles let their bangs
grow, stopped wearing suits with vests. Yoga and
Zen started big new waves. Many other inputs and
outgrowths can be named, all the way back to
the BEATNIKS. The newest big roller, I'm told, is
THE MOLE PEOPLE, who all wear black and come out
only at night. Wow! *That* close to ground, you're
under! . . . What if that's best? What if instinct
prophetically leads the young, and all of us, *under,*
deeper, darker, blinder, into the final womb?
While there's still time. Before the first launch,
which will be the only one.
No, that's the apocalyptic cop-out. Not true.
New Wavers, listen: (But they can't, they never do.)
Listen, there's just one "Don't," one "Keep Off,"
one "Keep Away From"—and I don't mean "the Grass."
It is: *Don't be a clone.* Don't do what the others
do. Because what they do, they do because others do.
It's good to be down there, level with nature,

like a plant, like an animal. Thoreau and
Whitman knew it. Gandhi in his dhoti felt
the magnetic pole of the earth. But, make *your own*
moves. Go opposite, or upside down, or Odd.
When everyone's odd, be the first to go Even. And,
on flipover, take the reverse course, of course:
In slow company, go fast; and in fast, slow.
With the ultra-slick, be rough; with the savage, noble.
Like Billy Budd, stay sweet: The arm that flogs you
will fall off. When everyone's on the joystick,
hunker down back home by yourself, with *War and Peace*.
Every one on the Orgasmatron? Be chaste. Then,
when they button, you can unbutton.
Not to be robotic, fix-focused on that straight
slit up the middle of some cat's eye. *Not* to be
either knee-jerked or Lotus-folded into the annealed
mob of spastic hot punk-rock clones, or else
upstairs among the pawky cornball Majority Morals.
Not needing to share, with identical nerds,
the pop trash, fake funk, sugar-diluted rush, *nor* prayer
in the schools. Get up, get out on the fresh edge
of things, away from the wow and flutter. Stand alone.
Take a breath of your own. Choose the wide-angle
view. That's something, maybe, you can begin to
learn to do, once you're *out* of college.

FOUR

COMICS

INNARDS

As many ripples,
loops and fingers,
kinks and pockets,
scallops,
curls and ruches
as the surf
on frilly waves—

          corrugated, convoluted
          slippery links and
          pinks and puckers,
          frothy overlapping
          fringes:

               Enormous
               Anemone!
               Look
               in the Anatomy Book:
               the spastic heap
               indented, redundant,
               crimped, voracious,
               over-abundant,

                    squeezing,
                    mashing,
                    munching,
                    pinching,
                    spitting

                        it out. The end?
                        No, still more
                        clench and squirm
                        and fretted froufrou
                        at each bend:

                            a bore,
                            the belly
                            a bushel

of tripe. I turn
to the velvet kidney,
the orderly heart,
liver and lungs'
aesthetic pattern.
They somewhat

       soothe the gripe.
       But it's hypnotic,
       that exotic page.
       Could I unravel
       the capacious

              maze, the conduit
              of travel,
              my future
              might
              come clear. It says here,

                    that *if*
                    I could uncoil,
                    could straighten
                    it, I'd have
                    a thong—

                          What
                    would I do
                    with it?—
                    25 feet
                    long.

THE DIGITAL WONDER WATCH

(An Advertisement)

When I look at the time,
it tells me the date,
the speed of my pulse,
my height, my weight.
It tells me how fast I'm
running, how straight.
It tells me my balance,
the dividend rate.
It tells me my birthday,
my license plate.
It's a wonderful watch!

Suppose I'm in London
and want to know
what time it is in Kokomo?
The weather in Miami or Maine,
how much sun or how much rain?
The name of the Daily Double to win?
Whether black or red
is the number to spin?
All I need to do is look at the time.
It's elegant, neat, the size of a dime.
It's a wonderful watch!

It tells me my shoe
and my collar size.
It tells me the color of my eyes.
If I'm lost in the woods
it tells me North,
phases of moon and tide,
and so forth.
It tells me how hot I am, or how cold.

It tells me I'll never,
never grow old.
It's a wonderful watch!

Does it tell when the world ends?
And when did it start?
Does it show how to wind up a broken heart?
Well, that's in the works,
and of course, it's true
there's still to be added
a gadget or two,
to warn of earthquake, volcano, or war,
and how long the sun
will exist as a star.
Yes, it's a wonderful watch!

THE GAY LIFE

(*to be sung*)

When there are two,
there will likely be
at least three:
the Mommy,
the Daddy,
the Ba-a-by.

Sometimes the Mommy
is the Baby—
sometimes it's the Daddy.
Baby can be Baby *and*
Daddy—in fact,
prefers to be.

Daddy can sometimes be
Mommy. But when
Mommy's Mommy, she's
not supposed to be
Ba-a-by.

Baby-Daddy prefers
Mommy to be Mommy,
although Mommy may
want to be
Daddy, or Baby, or
Daddy-Baby.
Daddy may let Mommy be
Baby-Mommy, but prefers
her not to be
only Ba-a-by.

Each can be,
in turn, Mommy, Daddy,
Baby—but not
simultaneously.
Two Mommies, two Daddies
or two Babies:
Misery!

Bad enough, if Daddy
is Baby when Mommy
wants to be—
or wants Daddy to be
just Daddy, when she
isn't—or Daddy wants
Baby-Mommy to be
just Mommy, and she
isn't, or doesn't
want to be.

Sometimes Mommy wants
Daddy to be
Baby, for now, for fun—
but then get up and be
BIG DADDY—and Daddy
won't be. That's bad.

Or, sometimes
Baby-Daddy wants
Mommy BIG. But not
TOO BIG. That's

82

too bad. Sometimes
there's just a Baby
and a Mommy.
Or a Baby and a Daddy.
That's bad, too.

Two bad is too bad.

Suppose there's just
a Mommy and a Daddy?
Fine. If Mommy will be
Daddy, and Daddy
will be Mommy *sometimes*.
It's likely each

will come to be
Baby sometimes.
That's O.K.

If there's a Daddy-Mommy
and a Mommy-Daddy, and
each wants to be
Baby sometimes, but not
at the *same* time—
that's good. That's
the way to be. Because
when there are two,
there will likely be
at least three.

FIT

Let's do one of those long
Narrow *New Yorker* poems to
Fit between the ads on about

Page 69. It should be fresh,
Have color and panache and
Make a few references to

Mainstream name brands,
Such as Sulka, Cuisinart or
Baggies—to fit with the ads,

Why not? "Original Baggies
Combine the loose fit of swim
Trunks and the roughness of

Rugby shorts. Reinforced side
Pocket, and nylon inner brief.
Colors: Red, Teal, Gold, Purp-

Le, Khaki, Marine Blue, Pea-
Cock, Silver." I want a silver
Baggie. Am ordering from Ven-

Tura, Ca., Box 3305, adding
$2.50 for postage. It needs
To be around 60 lines, spaces

Counting as lines. So, let's
Fit in a few frames by my favo-
Rite cartoonist: 1. Man asleep

In bed by old-fashioned alarm
Clock. Dog asleep in heap on
Floor. 2. Alarm goes off. Dog,

Cross-eyed, is scared awake.
3. Man in pajamas, brushing
Teeth. Dog scratching fleas.

4. Man, dressed, putting on
Coat. Dog just standing there.
5. Man, with briefcase in door-

Way, leaving. Dog just stand-
Ing there. 6. Door closed,
Room empty. Until we see

Lump in bed under covers.
It's dog asleep. Still too
Short? Three-line stanzas

Instead of four may make it
Fit. It's worth it. Here goes.
Poetry pays better than prose.

SUMMER'S BOUNTY

berries of Straw   nuts of Brazil
berries of Goose   nuts of Monkey
berries of Huckle   nuts of Pecan
berries of Dew   nuts of Grape

berries of Boisen   beans of Lima
berries of Black   beans of French
berries of Rasp   beans of Coffee
berries of Blue   beans of Black

berries of Mul   beans of Jumping
berries of Cran   beans of Jelly
berries of Elder   beans of Green
berries of Haw   beans of Soy

apples of Crab   melons of Water
apples of May   melons of Musk
apples of Pine   cherries of Pie
apples of Love   cherries of Choke

nuts of Pea   glories of Morning
nuts of Wal   rooms of Mush
nuts of Hazel   days of Dog
nuts of Chest   puppies of Hush

A NOSTY FRIGHT

The roldengod and the soneyhuckle,
the sack eyed blusan and the wistle theed
are all tangled with the oison pivy,
the fallen nine peedles and the wumbleteed.

A mipchunk caught in a wobceb tried
to hip and skide in a dandy sune
but a stobler put up a EEP KOFF sign.
Then the unfucky lellow met a phytoon

and was sept out to swea. He difted for drays
till a hassgropper flying happened to spot
the boolish feast all debraggled and wet,
covered with snears and tot.

Loonmight shone through the winey poods
where rushmooms grew among risted twoots.
Back blats flew betreen the twees
and orned howls hounded their soots.

A kumkpin stood with tooked creeth
on the sindow will of a house
where a icked wold itch lived all alone
except for her stoombrick, a mitten and a kouse.

"Here we part," said hassgropper.
"Pere we hart," said mipchunk, too.
They purried away on opposite haths,
both scared of some "Bat!" or "Scoo!"

October was ending on a nosty fright
with scroans and greeches and chanking clains,
with oblins and gelfs, coaths and urses,
skinning grulls and stoodblains.

Will it ever be morning, Nofember virst,
skue bly and the sappy hun, our friend?
With light breaves of wall by the fayside?
I sope ho, so that this oem can pend.

GIRAFFE

A Novel

CHAPTER 1

Giraffe is the first word in this chapter. Is is the second word. The is the third word. First is the fourth, and word is the fifth word in the first chapter. In is the sixth and this is the seventh and chapter is the eighth word in this chapter.

CHAPTER 2

Is is the second word is the second sentence in the first chapter. Is is the first and the second word in the first sentence in this chapter. The is the third word is the third sentence in the first chapter, and the third word in the first sentence in this chapter. First is the fourth, and word is the fifth word in the first chapter is the fourth sentence in the first chapter.

CHAPTER 3

The fourth sentence in the first chapter is in the fourth sentence in the second chapter.

CHAPTER 4

The first word is Giraffe, and the second, ninth, tenth, fifteenth, twentieth, twenty-fifth, thirty-fourth, thirty-ninth and forty-fourth words in the first chapter are is. In the second chapter the is the third word, and the is the fourteenth word in the third chapter. In this chapter the first and last words are the.

CHAPTER 5

First is the first word in this chapter. In the fourth chapter the fifth word in the last sentence is first.

CHAPTER 6

The fifth word in the fifth chapter is word and words is the fifth word in the last chapter. Words in the second sentence in the fourth chapter is the eighth word. In the second chapter word is the fifth word, the twenty-first word, the thirty-third word, the forty-fifth word, the fifty-eighth word and the sixty-second word. Word is the third word in this chapter, and in in this chapter is the fourth word in the first sentence. In is the sixth and this is the seventh and chapter is the eighth word in this chapter is the fifth sentence in the first chapter.

CHAPTER 7

This is the first word in this chapter and the third and seventy-fifth word in the tenth chapter. Thirteen words in the first seven chapters are this.

CHAPTER 8

In the first chapter chapter is the last word. In the last chapter the twenty-seventh word is chapter, and in this chapter chapter is the first and the fifth word in the last sentence. Chapter in the next chapter is the ninth word in the third sentence.

CHAPTER 9

Sentence in the third chapter is the third word and the twelfth word in the sentence. Sentence is missing in the first chapter. Sentence in the last sentence in the second chapter is the eighteenth word. Sentence is missing in the fourth chapter and in the seventh chapter.

CHAPTER 10

In in this sentence is the first, second and twenty-first word, and this is the third, thirteenth and twenty-second word in this sentence. And is the first and fifth and seventh and ninth and eleventh word, and the fourteenth and the seventeenth, and and is the twenty-first, twenty-second and twenty-seventh word and the thirtieth word in this sentence, and in this chapter the seventy-ninth word is and. In the first chapter in and this are the sixth and seventh words.

CHAPTER 11

Words in this novel are are, next, last, A, Novel, a, missing, novel.

CHAPTER 12

Three words are A, two words are a, three words are Novel, seven words are novel in this novel. Thirteen words are CHAPTER, two words are chapters and forty-six words are chapter. Fifty-one words are is and thirty-six words are are. In this novel forty-one words are and and one hundred and three words are the. Thirty words are first. Three words are next. Ten words are last. Twelve words are second, eleven words are third, ten words are fourth, nine words are fifth and three words are sixth. Seven words are seventh and four words are eighth. Sixty-four words are in in this novel. Twenty-eight words are this and twenty-three words are sentence. Four words are missing. In this novel fifty-one words are word and thirty-eight words are words. Four words are word in this, the last chapter. Three words are GIRAFFE in this novel. Three words are Giraffe. Two words are giraffe. GIRAFFE is the first word. The last word is giraffe.

FIVE

BANYAN

When "Beestes and briddes koude speke and synge ..."
—CHAUCER

I left my house. I went to live
in the house of the Banyan,
in the hush of space, in rooms of leaves.
A high round roof leaked ragged stabs of sky.
Chin on knees, I sat beside the wide pleated trunk
from which thick spokes of bumpy roots rayed out.
Their crooked hooks continued underground.
On a bare floor, but for brown dry leaves, I sat.
I was my own chair.
Swung a long arm up. My toes were grasping thumbs.
Asquat on the first smooth limb, I looked aloft
through scaffolds of layered shade.
I swung higher, and sat.
My lungs filled, I breathed cool mystery.
Such quiet aloneness enough for the first day. . . .
A broad limb that hardly steepened
its bridge toward the setting sun
became my couch for straddling sleep.
Soon the moon my bedlamp.
In transit, Jupiter and Venus lay out there
close enough to kiss. Or this was a dream.

The 2nd Day

Morning. I mounted higher.
I knuckle-walked an opposite limb. Twisting,
it trespassed a neighbor grove. I stole
a freckled fruit from the top of a bearing tree
that Banyan overstretched—yellow, shape of a small
football—bit it in half, sucked the sticky juice.
Inside were mucoid seeds, slimy, black.
The pulp was sweet.

Up high, my back to a central column, safe at home,
sequestered by leaves, at peace and belly full,
I began my survey. Stretched my short neck,
scratched an armpit, blinked lashless eyes
and stared around:

> Banyan from many elbows dangles strands
> of strong brown thongs. Long clean curling beards
> the wind swings. . . .

I yanked a handful of evidence, twirled and slid
neatly down. Hands are feet when need be, feet are hands.
Tail's an extra, a fifth. Can almost fist its ruckled end.
On the ground I found:

> Banyan's tough tassles grown long enough to touch
> soil, plant themselves, transform to roots. Roots rise,
> harden, become new trunks, fatten, grow limbs. Limbs
> branch, spread, intertwine and rise, thicken to GIGANTIC.
> Swollen coils could strangle Laocoön, his sons,
> and all his grandsons. . . .

Chin on knees, I crouched playing with a swatch
of Banyan's beard, the squared-off end like horsetail
hung a foot from earth, while other strands had rooted.
My eyes, nearly to the top of my forehead, stared
up at a monstrous muscular tangle. Squintholes in the roof
were squeezing shut. Was there a smell of storm in the air?
I imagined cloud-mountains swelling and fusing, black-veined,
writhing, the sky shutting solid. . . .

Suppose a great grove of mature Banyans replicating
without hindrance, reached out and down and up, invaded
adjacent trees. A wall of trunks, entwisted limbs, thick beams,
and underground, clenched roots upheaving. Suppose the process
speeded up: struggle causing need for struggle, need causing
need for accelerated speed. Suppose Banyan, a jungle, engulfed
and hugged to death all other growth on the whole peninsula.
Jammed together, a vast vegetable loaf, a dense choked block,
closed as rock, would leave no air, no egress, no exit. . . .
No house, no room, no breath.

I'd thoroughly scared myself. I lay down on my side,
and wrapped long arms around me. Curled tight in a trench
between the biggest roots, I fell asleep.

The 3rd Day

It rained in the night. A warm caressing rain.
I let it run its rills between my lips,
it washed and soothed my eyelids.
I awoke just at sunup, reached a long arm
to a new limb, climbed in a fast slant,
almost flying, and knuckled along a broad
limb that wriggled west. A path so clean and wide
I could have ridden it on a unicycle.
High off the ground the limb led deep
into the aerial forest. Although it was day
it was dark under leaf-roof dense and evergreen,
a blackish green like lizard's skin.
I ran sometimes, and sometimes swung along,
catching hold of the dangling tawny swags.
Looked down, saw gables and eaves depending
on pillars or shafts grabbed into earth below,
complex supports of the Banyan colony, a whole
estate. Tall circular uprights extending
from spacious arches were linked above by bridges,
balconies, tunnels, under-and-over-passes
which spread laterally and vertically, a labyrinth.
Unexpected, at a fork, an opening.
The broad path, the limb I ran on, swerved,
petered out to a narrower trail, and ended!
I sat on the point of a slender bouncing limb,
just now sprouting its first leaves.
Looking back, I saw the trunk this little limb
belonged to. Not a Banyan. A young Live Oak
appropriated by Banyan which, beginning at the base,

had trussed it round and round with cords and ropes
of vinelike roots that climbed the limbs.
Some trusses dragged the ground and anchored there.
The slender trunk, bound tight and squeezed,
awaited a dry death. The fragile top was green,
but I saw how the entire oak would be incarcerated,
killed finally inside the swelling base of a new
Banyan spreading skirts with heavy hems, merging
its roots and, from on high, slinging nooses
over the upper limbs of its prey, choking off
the sap, destroying it that way.

> Banyan, not from nut or pit or core nourished
> in earth grows up, but parasitic lives.
> Banyan exists and thrives by capture, torture
> and murder of youths, adjacent trees.

Then monster of trees! From such process
is beauty and wonder born? Does greatness come
from merciless exploit? Overwhelming evil then,
the campaign of Banyan, if its goal is gobble all
it can reach, to decimate its neighbor trees,
to leave no rooted trace of other body-shape alive
outside its own expanding torso. To combine,
for a solidarity beyond challenge, with ogres
of its tribe, to form a fortress lacking a single
slit through which a stab of death can creep?
Is this the goal of it? How and why occurs
the simultaneous spread—out and down and up at once—
of this necromancer, proliferating like a cancer?
I would find out.

The 4th Day

Not to cause commotion
in the library
with my sudden hairy
self, I had the notion

of slipping in when it
would show CLOSED FOR
HOLIDAY on the door.
So here I sit.

I can pick a lock
as nimbly as a nose, or spin-
ning number to win,
or wallet from a pock-

et, or latch on any cage.
Leathery fingers in a drawer,
I riffled cards for BAN, for
TRE. Finally found book and page.

Only after certain
gymnastics, scrambling up ladder, hand
over hand, to land
with—"Whee!"—swing of a curtain,

on high balcony shelf labeled
BOTANICAL REFERENCE A to Z,
was I to be
at last enabled

to read:

BANYAN. Greatest spread of any tree in the world. Height can be 100 feet. Aerial roots grow downward into soil and form thick pillars which support the crown. Single tree can appear to be dense thicket. Related to the Fig, which has similar unusual flowers and fruits. At the botanic gardens of Sidpur near Calcutta is a famous Banyan with massive main trunk twelve feet in diameter, and with huge additional trunks. The whole covers an area of 900 feet in circumference.

> I am crouched on a stool,
> toes wrapped round a rung,
> pencil in teeth, absolutely hung
> up on this fool-
>
> ish research. Of course
> I'm ill-equipped. The duplicator,
> like the elevator,
> is out of order. Worse,
>
> autodidact that I am, by book
> little learning found
> not sniffed out on actual ground
> or by firsthand look....

Well, to proceed:

BANYAN. Species of fig of the family *Moraceae* (Mulberry.) Held sacred in India. The seeds germinate in branches in some other tree where they have been dropped by birds. Young plant puts forth aerial rootlets which, on reaching ground, grow secondary trunks to support horizontal limbs. Branches from the trunks ultimately send down more prop roots, until Banyan crowds out the host tree and becomes grovelike. Covers large areas. Forms arbors. Seeds can germinate on walls and buildings, causing cracking, as with the Strangler Fig.

Reading these
words, I must have muttered
some when, harshly uttered
from below, I heard: "Quiet, please!"

Oh, someone's rage
I'd aroused. But I could see
no one. The command must be
coming from a cage

in the library's sunporch.
There it hung
and slightly swung.
Something like a yellow torch

I saw flip up within—
a feathered crest, wild
and spikey. A burst of riled
repeats: "Quite, please!" made a din

clear to the cathedral
ceiling. Two or three grabs
of the railing, and slabs
of the tall wall

of books, let me down. Landed,
I laughed and said, "Boo!"
to a White Cockatoo
in a bell-shaped cage. Two-handed

(or two-footed) and razor-clawed,
thick-beaked, sassy and young,
with a fat agile tongue,
her cloud-white body broad-

hipped, she had alert round
eyes with lids of sky-blue.
"I'm Blondi," she hollered. "Who
are you?" "Tonto." I found

my name invented on the spur.
"So get me out of jail!"
"Of course." Applying my picklock nail
to the latch, I freed her.

The 5th Day

We had gone far—far out, out on a limb,
Blondi on my back, beak clamped to my neck-hairs.
She clung to me, although we were not kin:
a coarse-haired Woolly Monkey ridden by a snowy,
silky, citron-tufted bird so purely beautiful.
Was she to be, by a flip of fate, my child?
Or mistress? Or mate, or other sort?
Anyhow, her mount. An unlikely pair. Where
would we go together? Wherever we liked,
it appeared. We hiked
our above-ground jungle, lost but entranced.
We tried every path. None led out. All led
in instead. Into the gnarled center
of Banyan's labyrinth. Was this the End,
this Center, the core of its initial trunk?
It had grown thicker, harder than before,
when alone I went to enter and explore.
The limb we stood on was wide as a sidewalk,
of smooth wood, high and curving, astonishingly
long, looping up and down and around, a good
fifty feet from the ground. And now, it
finally quit. Quit in the blind middle,
at a drop-off. Blondi hopped off,
as I sat upright. She came to my forearm,
walked to my shoulder, and tweaked
my ear. This time, with a tender beak.
A bit panicked, I complained, "What
are we doing *here*? Where do we go now, and why?"

"Go now," she squealed. "Let us go now,
you and I!" Her tone was mischievous. Mine
was annoyed. "What does *that* mean?" Sign
of my panic: "What does any of it mean?"
I leaned against a fork as into an armchair.
Blondi came to my knee. I continued:
"Where we are, where we're going, has to have
a purpose, doesn't it? If this is where we
live now, our house, our world, we need to find
some reason for its being—uh—as we find it.
Need to sense extension and geography,
some sort of history of growth and shape—
no matter how peculiar. To form a projection
of its future, don't you agree?"
"Birds in their little nests agree,"
Blondi sang triumphantly. Those librarians,
it became plain, had programmed her. Her brain,
although instinctively wise, had much to unlearn.
"Be serious for a minute, Blondi." My stern
suggestion went unheard. She squawked out:
"Whether thou choose Cervantes' *serious* air,
Or laugh and shake in Rabelais' easy chair ..."
Before she could say the rest, I pretended
a cuff up-side-the-head. Her crest
flared erect like a yellow tulip. She skipped
to a limb above me, rampant, incorrigible.
Ignoring her, I went on: "We citizens here
domiciled apparently by chance, *if only* bird
and beast—" I drummed my chest—"need at least
one absolute with which to begin to invent

a future. Some inkling, of how our wandering
is linked to an intent hidden in this snarled
enormous process, ought to surface here.
After that, there ought to appear
some sort of map showing where we're going
and how best to get there." Dropping to my lap,
Blondi with her claw-tip began to bubble my
lower lip! I grabbed both feet and let her
dangle, head down, like a caught chicken, while
I ranted on to the end of my speech: "We need
to see forward—I mean *toward* an Opening, and we
need to remember *backward* to Beginning—to
Seed and Root and Trunk. So as to foresee
the Fruit." She managed to screech, even from
her ignominious position: "The fruit of that
forbidden tree whose mortal taste . . ."
What a clown! I set her down, upright. This
baby wasn't dumb. She cocked her sunny topknot,
ducked and, suddenly, chewed upon my thumb.
"Ouch!" I hollered. "Gotcha!" she bragged.
"Gotcha! Gotcha!" The jagged
pincer of her wide hooked beak,
its underhalf a saw,
and her strong jaw-
hinge, like a bulldog's, could draw
blood. It could
refuse to let go.
Mainly, she was gentle with me, though.

The 6th Day

At first light exactly, Blondi climbed to a parallel,
slightly higher limb, stretched her glorious wings,
fanned them and squawked, "What's to eat? Blondi wants
a cob of sweet corn!" Saying this three times probably
meant she thought me a doubtful provider. And she had
only me. The security of her cage, her meals
provided in the library, had been left behind in order
to look for a better life. She could not fly. Both
wings had been clipped at the primaries. The best
she could do was to make short flaps upward, or brief
horizontal swoops. She had no hope of real takeoff.
In the high roof of Banyan were clusters of its copious
fruit, balls the size of small plums, claret red.
Like a streak I was hand-over-hand, and with nimble
toe-holds, up in loops and leaps, and when I slid and
swung back down, I had a branch ample with gay-colored
fruit in my teeth. In shade, at a fork I settled,
pulled off a "plum," licked it, let a tooth sink in,
winked at my pretty cockatoo. Maybe she'd bite and
taste. She did. From my hand she took and tongued
one of the red balls. Full of seeds, a bit grainy
and hard, but she liked it. She finished a bunch,
plucking each from its twig with her hooked beak,
dropping it into the palm of her "hand," her four-
fingered claw, with which she passed the fruit into
her mouth, cracking it in the hinge of her bone-like
jaw, letting the peel fall, swallowing only what
felt and tasted good. Finished, she pigeon-toed it
to a side-limb a little below me. I saw her flick
her short squared tail as she defecated, lifting her

wings away from her body. I saw how underwings and
tail hid hints of lemon matching the vivid yellow
of her crest when raised. On roost now, and at rest,
her eyes' blue underlids pulled shut from below,
her slate-blue beak plunged into the fluff of her
breast, her pate now smooth, completely white.
Odd how she could be so featureless as now, without
color, slick as a white wooden ninepin. Suddenly,
as like a Peeping Tom I peered from above, she stood
erect, stretched, spread wings and crest and every
feather lifted. A gorgeous fullblown snowy bloom—
a peony perhaps—she turned up for display all layers
of her pristine petals. Then, walking, hopping,
hoisting herself by beak, while mumbling rhythmic
squeaky comments—they sounded like staccato repeats
of "Oy, Oy, Oy!"—she managed to return to the wide
thick limb I sat on. Here she made a kind of toilette,
smoothing, arranging, placing each feather in its
alloted row with her beak and tongue. From a gland
at the base of her tail she brought tiny drops of oil
to groom her feathers. This kept them glossy and
impervious to wet or dust. The process took a long time.
I see just how it's done, was mumbling in my mind, *how*:

> Seeds of the fruit of the Banyan eaten by birds
> digested and voided, fall with their droppings
> to ground, are buried and sprout. Or, if left
> on tree limbs where bird has dined, they imbed,
> begin to grow and, in time, spill out a tassle,
> a rootlet that dangles down. That multiplies,
> lengthens until tawny aerial roots descend
> and touch earth. Triumphant then, a slim new
> shoot is born, destined to become a next great
> trunk as, earth-locked, it begins to rise.

Blondi was making sleepy croaks. Her blue lids creeping
up over her pupils finally closed. Dusk in the east,
Venus visible to the right of a sunken sun, and Mars
dim red, low to the left in the west, the myriad glints
of sky high in our capacious roof deepened their blues,
darkened toward black. I lay belly-down along my wide
limb, my tail coiled at its end around an upper and
slimmer limb—which was Blondi's roost. A Woolly's
tail has no fur near its end. Ridges of the rougher
skin on my tail maintained my grasp even when I slept.
My perched cockatoo, too, would be steady and safe
all night. Curved gaffs locked around the branch,
her weight hunching her down, her body kept easy balance
as she slept. I was peacefully thinking, drifting
toward sleep, how Banyan, our big house of eternal
summer, was a complete world we, perhaps, need never
leave. Lovely the fact that it remained ever green,
impervious to seasonal changes, long-lived, strong,
a giant close to immortal. . . . I slipped into sleep.

The 7th Day

A scream awakened me. High-pitched, ragged,
startling as a peacock's, as if rushing out
of the mouth of the sun itself.
It was only Blondi, crowing her greeting
to the day. Probably urging it to hurry
into full light. She strutted back and forth,
feathers fluffed, beak wide, fat dark tongue
arched, while sounding a series of trills,
clicks, whistles, croaks, mimicking other
birds she heard nearby and distant:
the Minah, the Macaw, a Spotbreasted Oriole,
a Bulbul, a family of Monk Parakeets and
a Forktailed Flycatcher. Using her beak
as a third "hand" she climbed on twigs up
limbs as on a ladder, and soon was high
enough to reach the Banyan's fruit by
herself. Following her, I saw her find
some dark ripe balls soft as figs, which
she rapidly relished. She hollowed the end
of her tongue like a spoon and scooped
drops of water from the folds and cups of
leaves, throwing back her head to swallow.
I breakfasted in the same way, except for
the use of different tools—teeth and
paws, and lips to sip with.
When we were satisfied, I presented my
back and the thick dark fur of my nape to
Blondi. Expert jockey, she instantly
grabbed and mounted me. We set out on a
new spur of our sprawling Banyan, pointing

east, but were soon moving up and down,
in and out in every direction.
Would we ever exhaust its possible paths
of exploration? It was one gigantic tree
at the same time as it was many.
Separated interconnected trunks constituted
a vast grove. Arbors had formed between
the side trunks, some of them fifty feet
or more away from the main where, below,
the root system like a wide skirt began
its spread upward to form buttresses.
Like columns and ribbed vaults and arches
of a great cathedral, the accessory trunks
helped hold aloft heavy horizontal branches
that, meanwhile, were extending and swelling
in diameter. I could estimate our Banyan
might be one hundred feet high and equally as
wide. At its widest it was a vigorous dense
thicket of glossy leaves completely hiding
the tree's armature, its trunks and limbs.
It was like an enormous closed rotunda.
Here was unique privacy, beauty, security.
It seemed one could live here—or two could—
free and happy to the very end of existence.
Banyan itself was virtually immortal. When
parts of the tree aged, younger parts would
simultaneously replenish.
My clever Cockatoo, too, had a parrot's
longevity. Studying her closely while our
intimacy grew, I could learn her tactics
of prolongation. I might live at least
a hundred years. . . .

"But why?" I heard my own
voice ask aloud. Blondi
on my back, riding me,
in the same tone

hootingly replied: "Why
or which or who or what
is the Akond of Swat?"
Undeflected, I went on, "Why

live long? Why does any thing
live at all? What's the purpose?"
"There's a porpoise
close behind us," she began to sing,

"and he's treading on my tail."
"Nothing behind us!" Monkey,
four-footed, neat as a donkey,
I picked the steepest trail,

where the windings of three
limbs, stretching up, became
contiguous, interlacing the same
way that a braid of hair can be

made with three strands,
the outer two brought under
and over the middle one—wonderful device. Setting feet and hands

into notches in the central braid,
Monkey managed to climb,
half a body length at a time,
up the pitched grade

that twisted and wound
in and out, until it bent
under like a Möbius loop, went
out, up and around.

I lost direction. Blondi's neck
swivelled like an owl's
as, with yipes and growls
of effort, we gained a sort of deck

high in the inmost dark
green heart of Banyon.
As in a corridor or canyon,
walled by thick leaves, rough bark,

although it was midday,
only narrow knife-glints,
mercurial flashes, gave hints
of light's entry a long way

away, or of any clear
exit. Blondi's luminous white
shape made possible my sight,
and just barely. Dear

Blondi, she was a lamp
of revelation, simply by her
being. My thick and dusky fur
assigned me the opposite camp,

of shadow, secrecy, obscurity,
I was nimble, determined, strong
in intent to unravel the long
mystery. But purity

of instinct and immediate act
were Blondi's way: simply *living*
life, not straining for reason, giving
and taking pleasure and laughter. Fact,

or the need to discover Source
of all exploding, expanding,
replicating Life, was not demanding
for her, of course.

"The one security we share
is Death," I told her.
Thinking I meant to scold her,
she snatched my hair

with a claw, yanked, and ("Ouch!")
put spurs to my hide
with her backward slide
off me. Rising tiptoe from a crouch,

erecting crest, lifting wings,
she was a wild and snowy bush
of feathers, to which I gave a push
with my snoot: "Of all things!"

"All things counter, original, spare, strange,
whatever is fickle, freckled . . ." Blondi picked up
the cue in operatic voice. She expressed
what she'd been taught, not what she thought.
Blondi could not, need not think. Her kind of brain,
of tongue, her genius for mimicry supplied the lines
that carried on the play, and fit the plot
coincidentally. Sometimes she proved prophetic.
In the almost dark we now stood on a sort of
platform, formed by the inner strand of the braid
of wide bark, just where it emerged from an immured
ancient trunk, perhaps the original stem of Banyan.
I had expected to turn a corner,
to find ahead, within range, a view
that would change the aspect of everything
so far seen and experienced—that would explain
everything, and show how it all combined as a Whole.
"We've looked here and there and everywhere
and gotten no closer!" I burst out.
"Who lives everywhere lives nowhere," Blondi said.
"What and where is the purpose?" I persisted.
"My purpose holds to sail beyond the sunset," she said.
"What if it's marked in the bark of this very trunk,
a sort of hieroglyph awaiting translation? What if

it's printed on my thumb?" I held up my thumb,
as if I could read the whorled lines. I collected
my tail and examined its rough end. The purpose
might be recorded by those ridges, being ready
for interpretation at mature growth.
What if the answer already belongs to me? I thought.
If inherent, then each of us already has his own.
If so, do we also need to know it?
"If an individual answer exists for each one,
what's to learn?" I asked this aloud, and Blondi
answered: "Learn of the green world what can be
thy place." Advice I could agree with.
"No overall true way? None to be found?"
About to tuck her head under a wing, Blondi replied
in a sleepy croak: "The true way goes over a rope
which is not stretched at any great height but
just above the ground."
If she and Kafka happened to be right, then
we were at the wrong altitude. I lay down on
the dizzy platform, drew knees to my chin.

The 8th Day

This day, which began before dawn, was spent moving from the dark twisted core of Banyan toward its edge, and down through endless tangles and tributaries of its thousand-limbed system. I moved in a trance, and Blondi on my back clutching my neckhair with her beak rode limp, as if still asleep.

We were both tired. What had happened at the top of the smooth center strand of the braid that issued from the knotted core of Banyan had been an emotional hurricane—at least for me. Blondi had enthusiastically mimicked my every reaction and gesture with full harsh volume.

Such a strange happening. . . . Had it been a dream?

A cage-shaped room, seeming transparent at first, was found to be reflective, a continuous wall-circling mirror. In the roof, a round opening which blades of lightning penetrated, dazzled and frightened us, igniting the room to platinum brightness. In the skyhole there appeared, floating—not clouds—what looked like chunks of ice, as if broken from an ice mountain, and there was a crackling sound like ice separating, under the growl and gurgle of water.

The "clouds" submerged and the opening turned black, glossy, a downsideup well, a depth without bottom. But since we were looking *up,* it ought to seem a vortex in the mirror-roof, tightening its whorl as it drilled higher. It widened suddenly like an eye's pupil, then narrowed, clicked closed. Again it opened, and lightning danced in.

A ring of images: of me, Tonto, and of Blondi beside me, leaped around the curved sides with the jagged lightning, finally subsiding to a standstill.

I had never seen myself. I mean, never myself standing *over there,* across from me—had never seen me entire, a whole creature. Had never seen my back, front and sides, and my face *all in one* at the same time, like this.

Opposite, in front of me was reflected a slim black Woolly Monkey covered with dense fur from the nails of toes and fingers to the eyes, mouth and naked ears, and from the top of the round head to near the end of a long prehensile tail. He had a doglike muzzle, somber deepest yellowbrown eyes, and the line of the lips curved up in a sickle shape.

Lightning spurted through the hole and around the cave again, and Blondi was swept into hoarse giggles and gusts of laughter. I shivered and whirled about. My fur stood up in a ridge along my back. I felt a strange electric thrill that made me whine, that bared my teeth. I paced four-footed right and left, nose to nose with myself. Strange, there was no smell.

The flickering ceased, but the intense light remained, turning the circular wall into a blinding sheet of foil. Finally the glare modified so I could see into it. Now two other persons stood reflected instead of Tonto and Blondi. I would rather not look. But I couldn't get away. Backing up, I saw a very old, naked woman backing up, stopped by the mirror-wall behind her. She was shrunken, her skin was sallow-gray and hung in pleats. Her stomach poked out and sagged, partly hiding her slumped, hairless pudenda, and her flattened breasts hung, the left longer than the right. Shoulders were narrow, upper back hunched, skinny neck and nearly hairless head thrust foreward. Arms and lower legs were thin, but the flaccid thighs, the buttocks and the coil of fat at the waist hung in jelly-like bags. Her body was spotted with warts of all sizes, some brown, others pink, and there were smaller hanging moles. Two moles hanging under her chin each had a coarse hair sprouting from it. Hands and feet showed purplish distended veins, and looked cold. The face seemed to have melted. Cheeks had slipped below the cheekbones. Pouched eyelids almost covered the slits of eyes. The left lid hung lowest—she could scarcely see from that side. Between nose and upper lip, the skin, dry and wrinkled, showed gray hairs that matched the frowning eyebrows. Her lips, string-like and crooked, pressed together sternly, and the mouthcorners hooked down to meet trenches of the slack jaws and corded neck. The chin, crosshatched and furrowed, had a few crimped hairs. Strangely, the forehead with its limp fringe of square-cut hair, was hardly wrinkled at all. Although the earlobes had lengthened and creased, the small nose, which was upturned with round prominent nostrils, remained inappropriately childlike. Once the flesh would have slipped entirely off her skeleton, she would not be quite so ugly: A frame of firm white bone, a delicate skull with empty eyeholes and fragile nose-socket, I foresaw, would be graceful compared to this dessicated body in its extreme old age.

The old woman wriggled her nose and coughed up a gob of sputum, munching on it while squinting back at me with a sour and suspicious expression. I looked down and saw, standing beside her, a child of about two years old, in a starched white dress. She was wearing black stockings and roundtoed black buttoned shoes. Straight, fine hair, blond, was cut square across the forehead above a tiny short nose. Rosebud lips were slightly parted in a tentative smile. A wide yellow ribbon bow stood on her head erect, like a whirligig. The child was pushing one chubby hand into a pocket of the home-sewn dress which was bordered with lace at hem and sleeves. A downy eyebrow, the right, arched a bit higher than the left, quizzically. Her narrow blue eyes held a direct look, confident and cool.

There was meaning to this vision. I could feel it. I understood. Whether real or dreamed, at the apex of our path, the limit of our search, there had been a signal confrontation. When the two images in the mirror vanished, replaced by a White Cockatoo with yellow crest and a grave-faced Woolly Monkey, I had said aloud, as if on some cue from the wings: "The purpose of life is to find . . ."

". . . the purpose of life!" Blondi interrupted in a shriek, making the intended question into its own answer. She did a wild pirouette. She had articulated what might be, I realized, a hopeless truth.

We were swinging down by my long arms from limb to limb. The limbs were wet, the leaves still held water, the wind blew. But the great storm had passed over. In rhythmically, gradually widening circles we descended toward the rosy, and then the gilded sunrise which mounted in the outer branches of Banyan. Our downswing took a long time.

It sometimes happens, when I'm carrying out some rhythmic, repetitious physical work, that words in cadence come into my head. As, with Blondi on my back, I dropped and ambled through the tree, my mind being immersed and haunted by last night's vision, I began to chant:

Small to great
Great to small
Robust to flimsy
Tiny to tall
Clear-eyed to blind
Fleet to stagger
Blossom to rot
New spoon dull dagger
Birthgasp to heartstop
Longing to lust
Flesh to bone
Bone to dust

Soon Blondi was saying it with me. It was she who had the notion of chanting it backwards, a variation which worked as well:

Dust to bone
Bone to flesh
Lust to longing
Heartstop to birth
Dagger to spoon
Rot to Blossom
Stagger to fleet
Blind to clear
Tall to tiny
Flimsy to robust
Small to great
Great to small

Our traverse of our green universe in its four dimensions encompassed miles—up, in, out, down. Banyan's growth and pattern, its evolution and expansion, although so intricate and immense, seemed blind. Maybe fortunate, I thought, because to have been foreseen and deliberate, stultified by logic, by aim and conscious end, would impose a fixed mortality, a necessity for extinction on this giant of nature.

Symmetry was everywhere avoided in its intuitive structure, and yet, unerring balance along with strength let it continually flourish. The many sidetrunks that had once been dangling tendrils, beginning their upward growth sometimes fifty or more feet away from the main trunk, propped up the increasingly heavy branches and insured that Banyan would survive the ravages of hurricane and typhoon. Roots of the main trunk, having attained huge size while the expanding limbs were buttressed by accessory trunks, allowed Banyan the greatest spread of any tree in the world. Its architecture, which appeared random, held endless delights and surprises, and especially an air of undefinable mystery.

Far out, on a whorled thick limb at the western edge of its boundary, more than three-fourths down its principal height, we rested. We had our supper of wild Mango, or Monkey Apple, the drupe of which is, in flavor and size, between a nectarine and a plum. Branches of this tall Mango tree penetrated among some of the lower limbs of Banyan. After sunset now, birds were floating in to nest in branches above us: the Monk Parakeet, Indian Mynah, the Bulbul, the Ani, the Stripe-Headed Tanager. Below in the twilight, a flock of Cockatiels skidded in to roost in Banyan. There followed three young Rose-Breasted Cockatoos. One wafted upward toward us, perched parallel, and stared at Blondi. How long since she had seen one of her kind? There was quick recognition. Instinctively she raised her crippled wings, stood up on tiptoe, and took off, intending to cross the fifteen feet between her and the birds. I had no time to catch her. She dropped, claws spread, mouth wide and tongue tolling, popeyed with terror, crashing through ledges of leafy branches. Grabbing at swags of rootlets, I raced to drop below her. A miracle that, in the near dark, I caught her in my arms before she could strike a limb and break her delicate bones. Knees bent, I put my back against a trunk, fisted the end of my tail around an upper limb, and cradled her against me, tucking her plushy snowy head under my chin. She whimpered and moaned, yet craned upward to where one of the Cockatoos had been perched. All three, of course, had soared out of sight—to Blondi's regret and my relief.

We would spend the night here, I decided. Blondi huddled against me, her pupils rolled upward, her blue eyelids raised and soon shut.

Now it was dark, a diamond-shaped opening in Banyan's canopy above us showed Jupiter in Capricorn still visible, but about to set. In Scorpio, Mars would soon rise, and then Saturn, while Pluto, always very dim, would not be seen until after midnight.

The 9th Day

The Long Night Moon at its most
northern point and fullest, 2:30 a.m.,
waked me, outlined every frond and stem
and swatch and muscular bough above, ghost-

white against black, a sky-wide X-ray.
The Long Night Moon rose below
us, swollen at horizon, climbing slow,
amazingly close, across a broad bay

gleaming in the east. Soon to land in the "real,"
having traveled what seemed a long
lifetime in a tree, a certain strong
fondness began to steal

over me for the old remembered scene:
my two-legged self walking the flats,
clothed like other thins and fats
who glide their rails of habit and routine . . .

". . . preparing themselves for life, which means a job and security in which to
raise children to prepare themselves for life, which means a job and security in
which . . ."

To slump back into the old halfsleep
of questionless existence? Live "as God wills"?
Just trust and be comfortable? Oh, rippling chills
ran up my spine! When would I leap

again into the arms of Banyan and,
swinging, let go, in free fall tumble, grab
a broad lower limb, land on its slab,
a smooth, horizontal, windfresh, leafy, grand

couch, or hammock swung among the stars?
Once I saw the thin old crescent moon,
Mercury and sparkling Venus strewn
in a magic diamond with ruddy Mars.

In silence so high on a clear night
like this, I felt I'd see to the edge
of Universe from my ledge.
Listening with held breath, I might

hear the faint first chime—
the soundwave starting to flow—
struck eighteen billion years ago
at the beginning of Time.

It was two and a half hours before sunrise when Blondi awakened. She did not
scream, but merely clucked and fussed and combed the feathers of her chest
with her serrated beak.

"Did you know," I said to her, "that our planet Earth and ourselves are made
of the same stuff that Supernovae once exploded into space?"

"Did you know, did you know," she said, "that Earth weighs six sextillion,
five hundred eighty-eight quintillion tons?"

"Exactly? My god!" I said.

"We are not to ask the mass of God," she said.

She's erudite and opinionated, I thought, possessing the rare genius-factor
of uneraseable memorization located in the hippocampus of some brains. But at

least Blondi is not a name-dropper. She never mentions the illustrious sources of her quotes. "Today," I told her, "Halley's Comet is due to appear, tail first, above the southeastern horizon just before sunrise."

She had nothing to say to this, to my surprise, but her round eyes with azure rims and unblinking pearl-gray pupils, seemed to enlarge penetratingly. It could be she had already seen Halley's Comet when it visited the solar system seventy-six years ago in 1910.

Moving to an outer limb with an open view of the predawn southern sky, we settled for the comet watch. Mars and Saturn were unmistakable, and the star Antares, in the eye of Scorpius, below Saturn. We had hoped for a bright swirl. What finally arrived was a tiny fuzzy circular blur, with a wisp of a tail leaning right, near the horizon. Miniature dim dustbull, or ice-pebble, it wavered there, hard to keep in focus, easily lost among millions of glittering stabs in an ocean of black. Until our star, the Sun, arose and swept the slate of heaven clean.

I stretched and looked around in the light, surprised at how far down we'd come by now. We could see the ground already, and looking east from the low crotch where we'd camped last night, we could see, turning turquoise in the sunshine, the wide bay, its beach closely lined with cedars and cypress. Fishing boats were anchored along its southern curve. Parkgrounds thick with palmetto and palm trees appeared below. With Blondi on my back, today a tranquil little jockey, we continued our spiral descent, meanwhile seizing for breakfast whatever fruit happened within reach. We found, in branches of trees that Banyan with its aerial roots had strangled and incorporated, some of the mucilaginous oblong orange balls, like large kumquats or small footballs, also eggfruits with sweet pumpkin-colored pulp. The polished pits like chestnuts were delicious.

I tried to recognize the paths of broad winding limbs and the shapes of ample forks, "rooms" we'd occupied or passed through in earlier travels. No, it wasn't possible. The scheme of Banyan was too large and complex. Or else we had not come this way going up. Or else the difference in angle of approach changed the view ahead. Parts of the tree would already have altered with new leaf growth, or changed with discarded branches after surges of storm. In fact, shifts of light and shadow, clouds, or winds were constantly altering shape and pattern, not to forget the changes of focus, of concentration and accuracy of aim, in the very lenses of our eyes.

Already we were down so far that through rents between branches we could see the splayed-out roots humped over the ground beneath the pillars and arches of Banyan, and the ends of long horsetails that, once they reached soil, would root themselves, widen, harden, become tripods, to form thicker footings that combined to make trunks of greater girth. The first impulse to growth for Banyan was not a stretching up toward light, but a groping down into earth.

I saw below, how an aerial root had dropped down and touched the top of a wide eight-foot wall of rough dark coral. It had snugged itself between the grooves outlining the stones and, where these widened, the root jaggedly swelled, snaking its way across and down. As some of the rootlets thickened, tucking between the sections of coral, they pushed them apart, splaying the crevices so that the wall began to break. I noticed how, at different places of the wall according to whether it was firm or crumbling, the descending roots accommodated themselves to the offered width and depth of inbetweens and, crimped or expanded, made their way over and under, extending on top or crawling along the border of the wall, until they finally reached soil in which to sink.

Pausing to rest and looking down, we found a stone gatepost draped in the several loops of an old tough Banyan root, convoluted, clumped and knotted, its heavy twisted length looking as if in motion. Of course it *was* in motion, so slow as to be undetected. Exactly like the coil of a boa constrictor wrapping the square wide post, it was the same grim color of old coral.

From above, seeing these signs of our approach to earth, knowing we were coming close to human properties and houses, the sun higher now, although it was still early, the light enlarging, scouring clear all the spacious rooms, balconies, rotundas, and the narrow nooks and mazelike corridors, bridges, underpasses of Banyon's every deck and story, I needed hesitation now—just now, when the possibility of camouflage was shrinking. I sat upright at a fork, shrugging Blondi off my back, offering my forearm to the double clutch of her strong feet. She brought her face close to me and rubbed her forehead against mine. She was mumbling, stammering something in a scratchy voice: "To find. The purpose of. Life is . . ."

Blondi was filing into memory, for future quoting, words of *mine*. I must get her home where she usefully belonged.

Continuing lower, we came to a place about twenty-five feet from the ground, where one of Banyan's offspring was trying to engulf an electric light pole. Limbs from a company of trunks on the other side of the road had crossed it above, building a leafy connecting arcade with branches joined and entwined which, duplicated and extended all along this highway, created a Banyan tunnel. Through this shady tunnel the auto traffic ran. It was six o'clock; people were already driving to work. Seated above them with Blondi, still hidden on one of Banyan's green balconies, I had the fantasy that, were the cars, one after the other, to stop below us, strong ropes of Banyan's beard dangling there might wrap around and lift each one, along with the passengers. Each would be bent, and crushed and thrust into the folds of Banyan's massive twisted trunks, which would swallow the cars, wheels and all, making them part of Banyan's expanding growth.

But it was time to exit from the tree while there was a chance of doing it neatly and quietly. I needed to get back undetected to my house on Flamingo Lane.

As Blondi trustfully clung to me, I jumped and gained the top of the electric pole, taking care to avoid contact with its wires that passed through a part of the cable-like strangler roots and limbs of Banyan. I handily spiraled down, using the cleats on the pole, crouching behind a trunk until there was a break in the traffic. I scurried across the road with Blondi, over the wall, into parkland, and then we loped along in the shadow of giant stalks of bamboo, flowering hibiscus trees and date palms.

COCKATOO MYSTERIOUSLY
RETURNS TO LOCKED CAGE

Coconut Grove, Fla., April 12—Ten days ago, Blondi, a white cockatoo, for many years an attraction in the town library, disappeared from her cage. Nothing else was missing, Marianne the Librarian reported. The empty cage was found locked, as were all windows and the front door. Yesterday, when the Librarian opened up at 9 a.m., she was greeted by Blondi shouting from her perch in the large hanging cage, "Quiet, please!" This phrase was the first her tongue had learned to enunciate clearly. She said it with startling authority. As Marianne delightedly approached the cage, Blondi rocked up and down on her perch and repeated her second accomplished line: "SH-SH-SH!" in a harsh whisper, while she lifted her right claw and held a tine against her open beak.

Marianne told *The Miami Herald* that she had no idea how the cockatoo got out, where she had been, nor how she got in again. "The cage is locked and unlocked with one key—mine—and it has no duplicate," the Librarian said. "But I'm glad she's back safe, and she seems fine."

The cockatoo has acquired new phrases during her stay outside the library, wherever that might have been. She repeated for this reporter a declaration she now pronounces often. Beak uplifted, wrinkled lids of an astonishing blue drawn up over her eyes, and with her lemon crest fully erected, Blondi the cockatoo recites in a pious croak, as if it were a poem:

> The purpose of life is
> To find the purpose of life
> To find the purpose
> Of life is
> The purpose
> Life is
> To find

Although born and raised in Utah, May Swenson has spent most of her writing life in and around New York City, except for visits to many states to read at universities and poetry centers, and she has traveled abroad in France, Italy and Spain. Swenson considers herself an autodidact, having never enrolled in a writing course or studied with other poets; nor has she affiliated academically as a teacher, other than for short stints as poet-in-residence. She earned a bachelor's degree from Utah State University, in Logan, in 1934. She was named an honorary doctor of letters there in June 1987. Among her awards are the Bollingen Prize in Poetry, the Brandeis University Creative Arts Award, Rockefeller and Guggenheim fellowships, the Shelley Memorial Award of the Poetry Society of America, a grant from the National Endowment for the Arts, the International Poetry Forum Translation Medal and a Bryn Mawr Fellowship. She is a member of the American Academy and Institute of Arts and Letters and a Chancellor of the Academy of American Poets.

May Swenson's poems have appeared in *The Atlantic, The Nation, The New Yorker, Paris Review, Antaeus, Poetry* and other magazines, as well as in many anthologies.

A NOTE ON THE TYPE

This book was set in Linotype Granjon, a type named in compliment to Robert Granjon, a type cutter and printer active in Antwerp, Lyons, Rome, and Paris from 1523 to 1590. Granjon, the boldest and most original designer of his time, was one of the first to practice the trade of type founder apart from that of printer.

Linotype Granjon was designed by George W. Jones, who based his drawings on a face used by Claude Garamond (ca. 1480–1561) in his beautiful French books. Granjon more closely resembles Garamond's own type than does any of the various modern faces that bear his name.

Composed by Maryland Linotype Composition Company,
Baltimore, Maryland

Printed and bound by Halliday Lithographers,
West Hanover, Massachusetts

Designed by Peter A. Andersen